AGVS at Work

AGVS AT WORK
AUTOMATED GUIDED VEHICLE SYSTEMS

Gary Hammond

IFS (Publications) Ltd, UK

Springer-Verlag
Berlin · Heidelberg · New·York · Tokyo
1986

Professor G.C. Hammond
Robotic Integrated Systems Engineering, Inc. (RISE)
Engineering and Education Consultants
1602 W. Third Avenue
Flint, Michigan 48504
USA

British Library Cataloguing in Publication Data

Hammond, Gary
  AGVS at work
  1. Automated guided vehicle systems
  1. Title
  629.04'9   TS191

ISBN 0-948507-23-3 IFS (Publications) Ltd
ISBN 3-540-16677-7 Springer-Verlag Berlin Heidelberg New York
                                 Tokyo
ISBN 0-387-16677-7 Springer-Verlag New York Heidelberg Berlin
                                 Tokyo

Phototypeset by Wagstaffs Typeshuttle, Henlow, Bedfordshire
Printed by Bartham Press Ltd, Luton

To my wife, Susan, who has operated our dairy farm and milked our 56 cows every morning and night, freeing my time so that I could write this book.

Acknowledgements

This book was made possible through the cooperation and efforts of many individuals. The author owes a great gratitude to several and especially to: *Robert L. Amans*, Senior Administrator, Automated Material Handling Section, Facilities Planning, GM Chevrolet-Pontiac-Canada (CPC) Group; *John M. Love*, Senior Staff Engineer, Facilities Planning, GM Buick-Oldsmobile-Cadillac (BOC) Headquarters; and *John R. Maicki*, Account Marketing Manager, Volvo Automated Systems for their invaluable help in obtaining material for critiquing the text and for making useful suggestions.

Thanks are also due to: *Jack D. Lane*, friend and partner in the consulting firm Robotic Integrated Systems Engineering, Inc. (RISE) for critiquing the text; *Gerry M. Drappel*, Manufacturing Engineer, Northern Telecom, Brampton, Ontario for helping to write Chapter Fourteen; *Robert J. McLendon*, Market Manager, TransLogic Corporation, for the information he provided for Chapters Eleven and Sixteen; *Carol Vargo*, for initially editing the text; and *Cheryl Holove*, who exhibited extreme patience in typing and retyping the manuscript.

Others who contributed photographs and other material include: *Ernest L. Young* of Litton UHS, *Kenneth M. Ruehrdanz* of Mannesmann Demag, *Mike Mrozovich* of Roberts Corporation, *Edward D. Back* of SPS Technologies, *Jim Arnsher* of Allen Translift, *Gregory J. Pachuta* of Control Engineering Company, *Robert A. Wolf* of Conco-Tellus Inc., *Michael Urban* of Mentor Products, Inc., *David J. Stankiewicz* of Elwell-Parker Electric Co., *Mark Holmart* and *Bruce E. Erickson* of Eaton-Kenway, and *Ronald Dix* of Volvo Automated Systems.

Many others contributed material for the case studies and are given credit in the text. Finally, thanks go to *Robert MacKenzie* of University of Michigan Hospitals, to *David E. Cook* of Westinghouse Furniture Systems, and *Brian Bennett*, Facilities Planning, GM-BOC Headquarters.

Foreword

Automated guided vehicles have been in use for many years. One of the first installations was a material-handling system installed in a General Motors facility in 1958. Sixteen years later the famous Kalmar Assembly Plant installed the first production system. This system was a culmination of efforts by many individual manufacturers, and has been very successful in proving that AGV systems are flexible, cost effective and quality oriented systems.

The industry has not stood still either. It has continued to expand and grow to meet the demands being placed on it by the using community. Our definitions of flexibility, cost effective and quality are continuously changing. AGV technology is also changing, and possibly it is this technology that is allowing manufacturers to redefine these concepts.

This book is an excellent starting point for the manager just being introduced to the world of asynchronous processing, or automated material handling. Gary Hammond's insight into AGV technology is straightforward, and should be considered a primer for anyone just discovering AGV systems.

I am sure you will find, as I have, that this book will not be the end of your learning requirements about the AGV industry, and technology. It is the beginning – and a good beginning at that. The concepts and principles presented should be read with an open mind – they are simply intended to be thought provokers.

Robert L. Amans

Automated guided vehicle systems are a United States development that have been widely adopted in Europe. The realisation that North American manufacturers must upgrade their facilities in order to improve their competitiveness in the global market has renewed interest in this technology back where it was invented.

The combined needs for a better working environment, increased productivity and quality, and an eye towards flexibility, make consideration of an AGV system almost mandatory.

This book is intended as a primer to acquaint the reader with the design, operating characteristics, and installation of guided vehicle systems. It outlines issues that must be addressed, provides suggestions of how to handle concerns, and showcases various applications.

Members of the AGV system supplier community know that a successful installation requires a specification drawn from a close working relationship between owner and vendor. This book may be used as an outline for developing an appropriate understanding between both parties and for writing the system specification. Manufacturing engineers and managers who are considering a change of material transport and conveyance methods can use the basic knowledge of AGV systems from this book to add to their evaluation.

John R. Maicki

Contents

Preface

We are living in the midst of a technological revolution. Historians and sociologists tell us we are evolving from an industrial society to the age of information. We are tying electronics to machines to create 'intelligent', 'automated' systems that perform many tasks which previously required human interaction. In addition, our 'shrinking world' is transforming us from a national economy to a world economy and forcing us to make present day decisions with consideration to the long-term implications of what we are doing.

Automated (or automatic) guided vehicle systems are an example of each of these trends. Originally developed in the USA as a tool for material handling, AGV systems have been adapted in Europe as movable assembly platforms that allow extreme flexibility, greatly improved ergonomics, and computerised control to monitor payload identification, condition and location. Not the simplest nor the least expensive method of transportation, AGV systems do require careful long-term planning to 'justify'.

This book draws on the experience of the author, of users in North America, and of AGV manufacturers who are applying this international technology in flexible manufacturing systems and automated material handling. It has been written for managers and engineers who are interested in AGV systems and their potential and current applications.

Chapter One is an introduction to what an AGV system is, the types of vehicles and applications in use, along with a brief history of AGV systems. Chapter Two summarises the advantages and justifications together with the limitations and negative considerations of using AGV systems. Chapter Three provides an overview of the types of vehicles, guidepath and guidance systems, and floor and system controls available to the user. Chapters Four, Five and Six give more details about the types of vehicles available, control considerations, and guidance and communication considerations. Economics and other justifications are discussed in Chapter Seven. Chapter Eight presents the reasons for system simulation including who should perform it, and Chapter Nine sets out the factors that should be considered when specifying a system. The steps for implementing an AGV system are covered in Chapter Ten, while Chapter Eleven presents an alternative to floor-operated AGVs – overhead AGV systems.

Chapters Twelve to Seventeen contain case studies of AGV systems in various industrial applications: material handling, assembly, electronics manufacturing, FMS, non-manufacturing applications, and heavy-duty applications. I was fortunate enough to be able to visit many of these facilities and to gain first-hand knowledge of the AGV systems. The personnel responsible for the AGV systems in a few of the facilities requested that they be allowed to write the section about their system. Those in other plants, besides showing me their facilities, provided the technical material from which I wrote about the systems. In a couple of facilities, I was shown the system but not provided with any technical material. I wrote about them based on what I had seen and was told. The few that I did not visit are based on technical papers and telephone conversations. In all but one case, the Volvo Components Corporation discussed in Chapter Fifteen, I had the written material verified by the facility personnel to ensure that it was technically correct. Each of these chapters also contains a section on special considerations for the use of AGVs in that particular family of applications. These chapters should reinforce the knowledge gained in the first ten chapters and give an insight to the advantages and problems the user can expect when applying AGVs to particular applications.

Finally, Chapter Eighteen concludes the book with a brief look at the future trends expected of AGV systems.

Gary C. Hammond
May 1986

Chapter One

What is an AGV system?

What is an automated guided vehicle system (AGVS) and why should managers and engineers be concerned about them? Like 'robotics', 'AGVS' has become quite a buzz-word in the present industrial revolution. Advancements in computers and other 'high-tech' automation devices, the need for a competitive edge in a world-wide market, concerns about the labour force, and financial concerns about high interest rates and long-term recessions, have all contributed to the new interest in AGV systems.

An AGV system is an advanced material-handling or conveying system that involves a driverless vehicle which follows a guidepath and is controlled by an off-board computer or microprocessor. Unlike other more conventional material-handling devices, such as Cartrac, roller, belt, or monorail conveyors, an AGV is able to select its own route or path to reach its destination. It has basically the same freedom as a manual fork-truck but does not require an operator/driver. Through its off-board controller, the vehicle is able to receive such dispatcher commands as identification of the load, its destination, and other special instructions. The controller, in turn, receives information either through a facility host computer or, in some cases, by manual input.

AGV systems were originally developed for distribution of materials in warehouse environments. Although this is still an important use, two major growth areas have evolved: the movement of material to and from production areas in manufacturing facilities, replacing manual fork-trucks; and the use of carriers for work-in-progress in assembly plants, replacing serial-type, asynchronous or fixed index, assembly conveyor systems. AGV systems are also used in offices to deliver mail, messages and small packages, in hospitals to deliver meals and laundry, and in 'clean-room' environments for material handling.

With increased pressure to automate factories, AGV systems have become the natural material-handling method. They can readily be made to interface with robots, automatic storage and retrieval systems (AS/RS), CNC machines, and all other modern forms of computer-controlled automation. An AGV system provides a material-handling system that is both flexible and readily adaptable to either production or product changes. The system, if properly designed, can be quickly modified or even expanded with a minimum of time and expense. AGV systems are now being used extensively in automated factories and assembly plants, in conjunction with other material-handling methods such as conveyors.

The growth rate experienced by the AGV industry is phenomenal, with sales in the USA tripling over the past five years. There has been a proliferation of vendors, each offering unique vehicle features along with different control and guidance approaches. Instead of offering a standard vehicle and controller, vendors are increasingly putting emphasis on customised vehicle design and systems that will meet the customers' specific needs.

Even though AGV systems were first introduced in the 1950s in the USA and later in Europe in the early 1960s, the technology caught on much faster in Europe. There are several factors that contributed to this:[1]

- The European work-force does not view automation so much as a threat since jobs are to a degree protected by government legislation (work-force reduction regulations make it difficult to reduce work-force size).
- European companies have standardised the size and construction of their pallets. There is no standard within most US plants, let alone a standard for the whole country.
- Longer-term payback periods are more acceptable in Europe, while companies in the USA look for short-term results.
- Stricter regulations with regard to safety and the work-place environment often necessitate automation regardless of the cost. (If improvements in the work-place environment and safety standards can be demonstrated, governments will often participate in the acquisition of automation.)

- A stable work-force, as found in European plants, tends to foster well-trained maintenance personnel and operators. (In the USA, the high turnover often results in inexperienced maintenance personnel. This leads to improper and inadequate maintenance, especially on advanced automation devices.)

Industry in the USA is now re-evaluating its situation and is making new commitments to advanced automation systems. Some of the factors contributing to this are:

- Foreign competition has become a serious matter.
- Vehicle and system developments made in Europe are now being transferred to the USA through a series of licences or ventures by European companies.
- The recession of the late 1970s and early 1980s was particularly damaging to the US automobile industry, forcing it to look for more efficient manufacturing and assembly techniques.
- The unions have adopted a new attitude toward the position of the labour force and are now looking for more job security in lieu of large salary increases. If job security is to be ensured, industry must compete successfully, thus more efficiency in production and assembly is needed. As a result, the unions are now much more receptive to the introduction of new technology.
- Development of vehicles with on-board microprocessors that can interface with other forms of advanced automation is concomitant with the 'modernisation' that USA industries are experiencing.

Managers, engineers, unions, and most of the work-force, all realise the need for an immediate improvement in productivity if industry in the USA is to survive. Most recognise that much of the improvement in productivity will come through automation; thus there is a growing acceptance of new technology on the part of everyone.

Types of vehicles and applications

AGVs are generally one of two types of material handlers: general material-movement carriers, such as tuggers or pallet trucks; and unit load carriers, used in production applications such as assembly, work-in-progress, or flexible manufacturing systems (FMS). A more extensive coverage of the various types of vehicles and their control systems is given in Chapters Four and Five.

Tugger vehicles

The first AGV systems developed were tugger vehicles, sometimes referred to as 'driverless' tractors, pulling a series of trailers
(Fig. 1.1). The major application for this type of vehicle is in a
heavy material-flow situation where the material is being moved
long distances and where there are relatively few destination
points.[2] Typical applications include moving spools of yarn, rolls
of fabric, and boxed material in the textile industry; and moving
incoming and outgoing materials between the storage area and
shipping dock in warehousing environments.

The AGV system selected can either be a 'closed-tow system' or
an 'open-tow system'. A closed-tow system is a dedicated
tractor-trailer unit in which the trailers remain attached to the
tugger. Usually these are basic point-to-point units and require
labour to load and unload. The loading and unloading may be
accomplished by hand or by means of a fork-truck, but in either
case it requires a worker or operator. These tugger systems have
the significant advantage that they can move a great deal of
material on each trip. However, this advantage may be offset by
delays if an operator is not immediately available to load/unload
the trailers when they arrive at their destination.

Fig. 1.1   Tugger vehicle and trailers

Two recent developments that tend to overcome this disadvantage are in the use of automatic load/unload trailers, and the use of an open system. The automatic load/unload capability allows the AGV system to transfer the load without an operator. An 'active' unit has trailers that are designed and equipped with a powered conveyor of some type that has the capability to move the material on or off the trailer bed. A 'passive' unit has a non-powered conveyor, such as a roller conveyor on the trailer, and relies on a transfer mechanism at the station to load/unload the material.

The open system is one in which trailers can be coupled or uncoupled either manually or automatically at the various destination points. The trailers can then be unloaded manually, as needed, by an operator. This feature greatly extends the flexibility of the system and lends itself to use in production facilities.

Pallet trucks

Like tugger vehicles, pallet trucks are for general material handling (Fig. 1.2). They are designed for situations where there is lower material flow over a moderate to long distance and with a larger number of destination points.[2] Pallet trucks provide an alternative to open tugger systems, especially where the material-flow volumes are lower.

Fig. 1.2　Pallet truck

The original systems required an operator at the destination points to drive the pallet truck to pick up or deposit the load, in the same way as using a normal fork-truck. In such a system, the operator, after picking up or depositing the load, programs the pallet truck for its next destination point. Upon reaching its destination, the pallet truck lowers its pallet to the floor and waits for the next operator. As with a manual closed tugger system, if an operator is not immediately available, there will be delays and inefficiencies in the system operation.

The first pallet trucks were limited to raising the pallet from 4 to 8in. (approx. 10–20cm), thus floor-to-floor movement was all that was permissible. Newer models can now lift loads 40in. (approx. 1m) or more allowing the pallets to be moved to or from most conveyors, stands, and racks, as well as from the floor. Also, pallet trucks can now automatically reverse so that pick-ups and deposits can be made automatically, increasing the efficiency of the operation. Another improvement is that some pallet trucks can be programmed to leave the guidepath at a certain point, find their destination, pick up or deposit a pallet, and then return to the guidepath for the next assignment.

Fig. 1.3 Automated industrial high-lift truck

A vehicle similar to the pallet truck is a unit that has high-lift capabilities. Whereas a pallet truck is limited in lifting height to about 40in. (approx. 1m), an 'automated industrial truck' (Fig. 1.3), or 'high-lift truck' may be able to reach as high as 19ft (approx. 5.8m) for placing material in high-rise racks. These vehicles usually have straddle arms for stability, although some have a counter-balanced construction.

Unit load carriers

Although a much later development than AGV tuggers, unit load carriers are becoming the most popular of the vehicle designs (Fig. 1.4). The vehicles are built to carry a single or multiple load on the deck of the vehicle itself. They are usually bidirectional, in that they can travel either in a forward or reverse direction along the guidepath. Some are also capable of sideways travel. These carriers have a high degree of manœuvrability, including the ability to rotate 360° in areas not much greater than the vehicle itself and the ability to travel in tight areas such as narrow aisles.

The deck of the unit load carrier is the work platform. For material-handling operations, the deckway consists of either an active or passive conveyor, such as a roller conveyor. It may also

Fig. 1.4   Unit load carrier

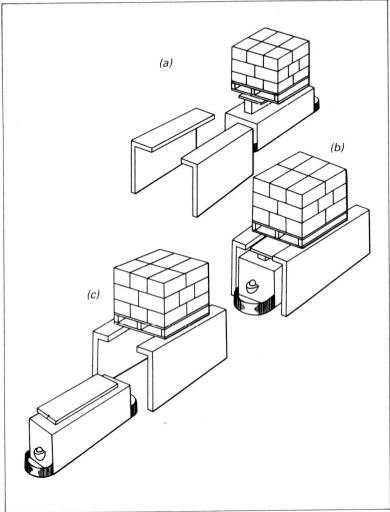

Fig. 1.5   Load/unload steps for lift/lower deck vehicles: (a) vehicle enters stand with load in raised position; (b) vehicle lowers its table depositing the load on the stand; and (c) vehicle exits leaving the load

be a lift/lower deck so that the unit load carrier can drive into a stationary stand, lower the deck and deposit the load, and then proceed onto the next assignment. Fig. 1.5 illustrates the load/unload steps for lift/lower deck unit load carriers. The major applications for these types of material-handling unit load carriers are in areas where there is medium throughput with multiple stops. Random material movement such as feeding line stock to manufacturing areas would be a good application.

The unit load carrier has also become an important component in assembly and FMS. In these applications the deck becomes the work platform for work-in-progress parts and assemblies. Instead of serial-type assembly lines, such as monorails, asynchronous assembly operations are possible with an AGV system. This allows operators to take more responsibility for the total assembly and to work more at their own pace. Also, if rework or repair is needed, the component can be shuttled through the repair station while remaining on the same vehicle. For FMS applications, unit load carriers can be designed and built with transfer mechanisms to move fixtures, tooling, and parts from workcell to workcell as required.

AGV systems are being integrated with other types of automation, such as robotics, CNC machines, automatic inspection stations, mini AS/RS and assembly systems in 'factory of the future' concepts. The flexibility, adaptability, and manoeuvrability of the unit load carrier make it a desirable choice for advanced manufacturing environments.

Historical development

The first AGV systems were developed in the 1950s by Barrett Electronics, USA. These systems were designed for simple material handling in warehousing environments and were based on basic techniques of wire guidance similar to those still used today. The control system was based on vacuum tube technology and was both bulky and relatively inflexible. The vehicles were of the tugger or 'driverless tractor' type, and were used to pull a series of trailers.

Three companies, Barrett, Jervis B. Webb, and Clark, competed over the years with the tugger systems. However, they received poor acceptance in the USA, especially by the industrial work-force. The unions saw them as a direct threat and even resorted to sabotage of AGV systems. Also, the vendors tended to offer only standard product lines and were reluctant to customise vehicles or controllers to meet customers' specific needs.

Advancements in technology have added to the growing acceptance of AGV systems. In the late 1950s, transistor technology replaced the vacuum tubes, making the controller systems less bulky, more reliable, and at the same time, increasing their capabilities. However, even transistor technology was too expensive for complex manufacturing material-handling problems experienced in industry.[3]

In the late 1970s, integrated circuit (IC) technology was adapted, which allowed for the development of sophisticated controllers. Also, during the same period, microcomputers were placed on-board vehicles, thus producing 'smart' vehicles. This allowed vehicles to determine their own routes to the designated destinations and control many vehicle functions, such as the work platform load/unload, raise/lower, rotate, etc. Likewise, the system controller was getting much more complex, to the point that it was able to interface with conveyor systems, AS/RS, robots, CNC machines and a multitude of other automation devices. Remote-location devices could call for vehicles and the system controller would dispatch the appropriate one, giving it all the pertinent information necessary to handle its load. Material could be tracked throughout the facility, giving a much improved method of inventory control.

One major reason for the new interest in AGV systems is the heavy influence of European applications and supplies. In the USA most developments were used to improve and enhance material-handling applications in warehousing, while the Europeans concentrated on developing unit load carriers from the towing vehicle. In the 1970s in Europe, light-duty vehicles (unit load carriers) were developed to replace line conveyors in assembly operations. Instead of a facility having a few material-handling vehicles, such as tuggers, the assembly plants are now using several hundred vehicles, such as unit load carriers, for work-in-progress operations.

In summary:

An AGV system is a high-tech material-handling system that involves a driverless vehicle following a guidepath and controlled by a computer. Unlike other more conventional material-handling devices, an AGV is able to select its own path to reach the designated workstation. AGV systems were originally developed for warehousing applications. From this, two major growth areas have evolved: firstly, in the use of AGVs for moving material to and from production areas, replacing fork-trucks; and secondly in the use of carriers for assembly work-in-progress, replacing synchronous (serial-type) assembly conveyor systems.

Industry in the USA is recognising the need for improved productivity and is committing itself to high-tech automation systems. Pressure to automate factories has made AGV systems the natural material-handling method. The growth rate of the AGV industry is phenomenal. Sales in the USA have tripled over the past five years.

Material-handling AGVs are classified into one of two general types: general material-movement carriers such as tuggers and pallet trucks; and unit load carriers used in production applications such as FMS. Tugger vehicles are practical for use in heavy material-flow situations moving long distances with relatively few stops. Pallet trucks are similar to tugger systems, but are used for lower material flow over moderate distances with a greater number of destination points. Unit load carriers are built to carry loads on the deck of the vehicle itself to the various workstations. The flexibility, adaptability, and manœuvrability of the unit load carrier makes it the most suitable choice for advanced manufacturing environments.

Chapter Two

Why use AGVs?

A lthough AGV systems have been in existence for over 30 years, they are only now coming into prominence. In the past, both manufacturing environments and labour and management attitudes made conventional material-handling conveyor systems, such as roller, power and free, monorail, and Cartrac, more feasible. Even today, in manufacturing environments where high throughput along with large in-process inventory buffers are experienced, the best choice may still be one of these material-handling systems. However, changes in attitude amongst employees and management, along with new automatic manufacturing techniques and the need for greater flexibility, have made AGV systems very attractive. This chapter details several reasons for selecting and justifying an AGV system. It also gives negative considerations and limitations so that a fair evaluation can be made.

Advantages and justifications

Reduction in labour force. An AGV system can increase the material-handling capabilities of a facility and at the same time does not require an increase in manpower resources. (It may even permit a reduction in the labour force.) This will result in a more stabilised labour force for peak-production periods as well as low-production periods (recessions or off-season situations). The labour-force reduction not only applies to fork-truck operators and other material handlers, but also clerks who handle material inventory and dispatch. Much of this type of work can be accomplished by the system controller in conjunction with the facility's host computer.

Improved productivity and quality. AGV systems have the ability to support asynchronous 'stop-and-go' types of assembly and processing. At present in many assembly-line environments, operators have to walk with and work on the workpiece as it continues moving. If the workpiece can be presented to the worker in a stationary manner, walking time and worker fatigue are reduced. This helps eliminate mistakes and improves craftsmanship and quality. For example, an engine dress assembly plant of one US auto manufacturer was converted from a monorail system to an AGV system, used in an asynchronous mode, and achieved a 30% reduction in demerits on the finished product.

Another advantage of asynchronous assembly for operations dealing with products involving a large number of options is that line balancing is much easier to achieve. Again this can reduce the labour force by eliminating inefficiencies due to poor line balancing. An AGV system can out-perform conventional methods because of better control over the vehicles.

Job enrichment and worker satisfaction. AGV systems used in the asynchronous mode provide a stationary work platform, as compared to non-stable, swinging monorail conveyors. Furthermore, the work platform can be programmed to lift and rotate, making the workpiece more accessible and reducing stress and strain on the workers. The system can operate at the worker's pace, which is not possible in serial or synchronous operations. This encourages the workers to take more responsibility for quality, which in turn enhances worker pride. Other incentives can also be given, such as the ability to leave work early when the work quota has been completed.

Another consideration is that the noise-level reduction resulting from the use of battery-operated (electrical drive) vehicles improves the working environment. Finally, parallel workstations can be designed into the system to promote team-building concepts. All these factors promote worker satisfaction, increasing retention rates, and thus reducing recruitment and retraining costs.

Real-time control of material handling. Material can be identified with the vehicle carrying it, providing the link for real-time tracking. The data can be transferred to the facility's host computer to support advanced material-resource planning. The resultant advantages are numerous, and include:

- Accurately maintained work-in-progress inventory.
- Reduced floor stock and delivery time.
- Reduced paperwork and clerk time.
- Reduced time-lag for information updating.
- Reduced waste material.
- Reduced inventory costs.
- Rapid response to manufacturing demands.

Reduction in space requirements. An increase in available production floor-space can be realised as a result of better work-in-progress inventory and rapid response, permitting reduced line stock in production areas. AGV systems leave an open aisle that can be used by other types of traffic. Because of their tighter tracking characteristics, they can be used with aisle clearances of as little as 1 or 2 in. (approx. 2.5–5 cm). Another important consideration is that the same guidance and control system can be used to distribute raw material, provide work-in-progress, and transport finished goods. With proper design, it is conceivable that the same vehicles could be used for all three functions.

Reduction in product damage. Material being transported by an AGV system is handled in a controlled manner which reduces material damage. Instead of being transferred from one conveyor system to another by workers or hard automation, the workpiece can be assigned to a vehicle. It remains with that vehicle even through certain operations, such as repair stations, that would normally remove it from the line. Asynchronous operation also permits a higher quality product by ensuring that it is ready for the next station. For example, all necessary components that are scheduled to be installed at a workstation will be installed. This provides for less chance of product damage at the next station.

Improvements in housekeeping. Housekeeping and safety are greatly improved by the elimination of other types of conveyors, such as floor conveyors, which tend to accumulate contaminants and waste.

Ease of removal and relocation. AGV systems can be installed relatively quickly and, with the exception of the guidewire, are easily removed. The vehicles and controls (the expensive portion) can easily be salvaged. Basically, only the guidepath portion is lost, the cost of which is relatively low. Since AGV systems are portable, they can readily be moved from one plant to another or from one location to another within the same facility. In one US auto plant, even though the facility was scheduled for a complete rebuild, an AGV system was installed in the engine dress assembly operation as a pilot scheme for learning experience. The AGV system was able to be removed and relocated in the new facility with relatively little expense; conventional material-handling systems would have been sold for scrap in such a situation.

Integration with other types of automation. Since an AGV system is a computer-controlled system, it is possible to integrate the AGV control with the controller of an FMS, for example a host computer. In CNC operations the host computer can link CNC machines to the AGV system to control and track the flow of material and to ensure the right CNC program for the workpiece being presented. The flexibility of an AGV system makes it one of the best methods for tying 'islands of automation' together.

It is possible to tie an AGV system to other automatic forms of material handling, such as an AS/RS, and to synchronise the activities of both. AGV systems are easily interfaced to other automatic devices to perform the following activities:

- Open and close automatic doors.
- Cross drawbridges.
- Use elevators.
- Provide automatic load/unload operations.

System adaptability and flexibility. It is relatively inexpensive to modify or expand an AGV system, whereas modification and expansion of fixed equipment, such as in-floor tow lines or conveyor systems, is difficult, time-consuming and expensive. However, for this to be true, the AGV system must be designed to accommodate a changing environment. This adds considerable cost to the initial outlay for the system. If this flexibility is not originally designed in, the AGV system may be no more flexible than any other system.

By cutting a slot in the floor and inserting the guidewires, the guidepath can be quickly modified or expanded at low incremental costs. Also, to expand the system's throughput, more vehicles can be readily added. (It must be remembered that the software has to be altered to accommodate the guidepath modification or vehicle additions. This can take longer than the physical revisions.)

Contributing to the system flexibility is the fact that the vehicles can be fully automatic and even, in some instances, leave the guidepath to perform tasks. Since they operate on self-contained power (battery), they move about more freely than most other material-handling devices.

This flexibility helps to resolve scheduling and sequencing problems and permits quick reaction to product changes and customer demand cycles.

Other considerations. In addition to the advantages already outlined, AGV systems offer other unique benefits, notably:

- Meeting the highest of clean-room environment standards.
- Providing additional opportunities to the plant's operation because of the system flexibility and adaptability.
- Improving competitiveness.
- Serving as a major element in equipment/plant modernisation.

Disadvantages and limitations

No matter how 'marvellous' an automation device may be, there are always associated drawbacks. AGV systems are no exception. In some instances these drawbacks may prevent a system from being installed or necessitate extensive modification of the existing facility to permit use of the device. Negative management and/or employee attitudes should be considered as a possible drawback. The purpose of this section is to present to the manager or engineer the other side of the picture, so that a fair evaluation can be made.

Expense. A well-designed AGV system, that will permit the factors listed in the advantages and justification section, will be expensive. Experienced users claim that the initial investment for large assembly-type AGV systems may be two to three times that of conventional material-handling methods. At the same time, they claim a maximum labour saving of only 10–15%. Other users, such as those using small material-handling AGV systems, have experienced payback periods of less than one year. Each system is dependent upon several variables, some of which are unique for any given facility; and it is often these unique factors that may justify the expense of an AGV system. It is usually easier to justify a system economically for a new facility rather than converting an existing one.

External use. In particularly cold regions outside usage is difficult. The guidepath must be kept free from snow and ice without the use of salt – salt can be absorbed in the surface (concrete, etc.) and erode the guidepath wire, causing possible shorting. Thus it is especially important that all vehicles used outside are made waterproof.

Floor surfaces. Vehicles are not designed to work on all types of floor surfaces. Floors that are dirty or that have extremely uneven surfaces do not work well. AGV systems can be made to work on asphalt, tile, and also wood-block floors if special installation precautions are taken.

Guidepath bed stability. Outside surfaces, such as concrete or asphalt, will heave with frost. Likewise, wood-block floors shift. The shifting or heaving experienced will tend to damage the guidepath wire, thus increasing maintenance requirements.

Metal floors. For most AGV systems, if a metal floor-plate must be crossed, it needs to be less than 16–18 in. (approx. 40–46 cm) in width. With greater distances, the vehicle will lose track of the guidepath and will shut down. For systems designed to leave the guidepath, the vehicle can be programmed to cross the metal floor and relocate the guidepath.

Management support. Will management support an AGV system after installation? A commitment by management must be made to support adequate maintenance training and to provide at least one maintenance person per shift. Another necessary commitment is to allow sufficient time, material, and personnel to troubleshoot and debug a new installation. The author is familiar with one installation where the divisional headquarters designed an AGV system for one of its plants. The plant management had little if any interest in seeing the system operate. Workpieces were not provided in order to debug the system, nor did they provide any support personnel. The plant simply worked around the AGV system. Since there was not a commitment on the part of the plant management and personnel, the system, although well-designed, was doomed to failure.

Worker attitudes. Not only must management be committed to successful system implementation, but equal support from the work-force is also necessary. Many of the early AGV systems installed in the USA failed because the unions saw them as a direct threat. Systems were forced out because of sabotage by employees. To minimise such negative attitudes, it is important to involve the user groups in the planning and configuration stages.

Obstructions. In many manufacturing plant environments, line stock, work-in-progress, empty containers, etc., are all stored in aisles, making it difficult for fork-trucks to manœuvre. Such practices, if allowed to continue after an AGV system is installed, will bring the entire system to a halt. (It is often difficult to break old habits, especially ones that have been practised for years.)

Ramp gradients. Ramp gradients are usually limited to 4–6%, although gradients of up to 10% are permissible with reduced load capacity. Long ramps may create such problems as overheating of motors and may further reduce the load capacities. In addition, if the vehicle is required to stop on the ramp (either emergency or programmed stop), the motor may not have sufficient restart power.

Maintenance. AGV systems are much more complex than other types of material-handling device and are thus more prone to equipment failure.

Other considerations. Besides the disadvantages and limitations already presented, other considerations are:

- The vehicles must not be used for inventory storage or act as buffers (vehicles are too expensive to act as storage racks).
- Vehicles for loads greater than 10,000lb (4536kg) are expensive and hard to justify.
- Load size and weight are important considerations.
- It is not possible to operate vehicles made by different manufacturers on the same guidepath and control system.
- Vehicles are not well suited for situations where the ambient temperatures will exceed 120°F (49°C).
- Sufficient lead-time (8–18 months depending on the system complexity) is necessary.

- It is difficult to upgrade a simple system into a complex one.
- AGV systems have low index-times compared to other types of conveyance systems.

In summary:

When considering whether to use an AGV system, both the advantages and disadvantages must be considered. Some positive aspects of AGV systems include reduction in labour force, improved productivity and quality, and worker satisfaction. AGV systems also provide for real-time control of material and less product damage. Their ability to work in limited space, to be easily relocated, and their ease of adaptation to other types of automation make AGV systems flexible.

Negative considerations include physical drawbacks of the system as well as management/employee negative attitudes. Many drawbacks are associated with the guidance system limitations due to floor surface quality and stability. Aisles must be kept clear of obstructions and ramp gradients limited to 4–6%, with reduced load capacity. Other major drawbacks include long engineering lead-times and the expense of AGV systems as compared to other material-handling methods. Also, the use of a higher level of software and hardware prevents the majority of electricians from troubleshooting and repairing AGVs.

Chapter Three

AGV system components

Although all AGV systems are different, they consist of similar components. However, the differences are sufficient to prevent the user using components from one vendor with those from another. For example, it is not possible to use vehicles from one vendor on another vendor's guidance and control system. This chapter is designed to give an overview of the types of component supplied by various vendors and explain some of the differences that prevent mixing of the components. It will also give some insight into the advantages and disadvantages of the various types of component. This should help managers and engineers to select the system that best meets their needs.

Vehicles

The component of an AGV system that is most readily identified is the vehicle itself. AGVs are driverless, battery-powered vehicles with reprogrammable capabilities for path selection, positioning, and a variety of different tasks. This is accomplished through either PROM exchange or image downloading. Vehicles are equipped to follow a guidepath system which can be easily modified or expanded.

The vehicle consists of the frame, batteries, on-board charging unit, electrical system, drive unit, steering, precision stop unit, on-board controller, communication unit, safety system, and work platform (Fig. 3.1).

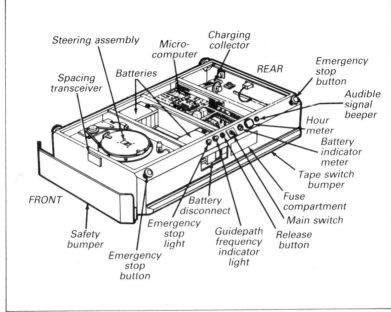

Fig. 3.1   Major vehicle components

Frame

The frame is usually constructed of welded steel members with aluminium cover plates. Since most vehicles have no suspension system there is a need for a level floor along the guidepath. (If the steering antenna jumps a few inches off the guidepath, the vehicle could be 'lost' from the system.) Manufacturers are hesitant to install a system on a wood-block floor, preferring concrete floor installations.

Batteries and charging

AGV systems are typically powered by 24 or 48V dc industrial batteries. These vary in amp-hour rating according to the installation requirements. Battery charging is usually accomplished by one of two techniques: opportunity charging or full-cycle charging.

The opportunity-charging technique involves the batteries being charged while the vehicle is performing or waiting to perform a task. Stations at which the vehicle is required to stop for any extended period of time become possible charging stations.

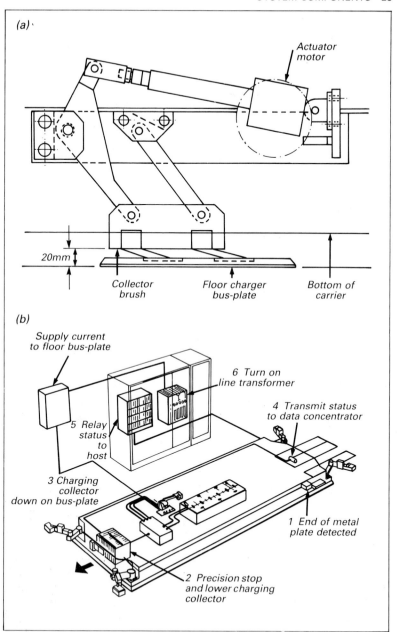

Fig. 3.2   Opportunity charging: (a) charge collector unit and (b) control system for charging

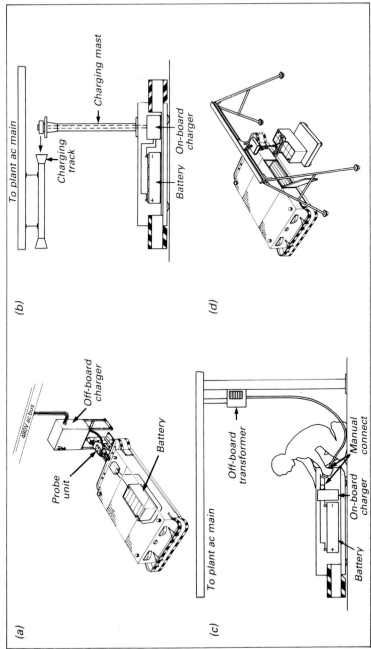

Fig. 3.3 Methods of full-cycle charging: (a) probe-type charging; (b) bus-bar charging; (c) manual/plug-in charging; and (d) change out

The charging collector mounted on the vehicle lowers the collector brushes to contact the floor-charger bus-plate (Fig. 3.2a). The vehicle then communicates to the floor controller that it is ready for charging (Fig. 3.2b). Once charged, and before the vehicle leaves that station, it communicates a request for the charger to be turned off and then retracts its collector brushes. This charging method permits the use of regular automotive maintenance-free batteries, since they are continuously being recharged. The technique is usually limited to AGVs used in FMS or assembly operations.

The full-cycle charging technique requires the AGV to pull itself out of service and into a designated battery-changing or charging area. This is done when the battery is nearly depleted of its charge. Several possible charging methods exist for full-cycle systems. Fig. 3.3a illustrates a vehicle driving into a probe unit containing the proper charging voltage; the voltage is produced by the off-board charger. Fig. 3.3b shows a vehicle inserting its charging mast into the charging track (the track is connected to the plant ac main), and Fig. 3.3c shows a manual plug-in type charger. Although it may be permissible for the AGV to be out of service for a one- or two-shift operation, it would not be acceptable for a three-shift operation where the vehicles are required to be in

Fig. 3.4 Battery exchange

continuous service – in this case a manual battery exchange is the best choice (Figs. 3.3d and 3.4). (Spare battery packs are much less expensive than spare vehicles.) All full-cycle charging methods require specially designed batteries, and the technique is normally used for tugger, fork-truck, or unit load carriers in material-handling situations such as warehousing.

Full-cycle systems usually require at least 17-hour batteries to provide two-shift service in a manufacturing environment. These batteries generally require four hours to charge, followed by a two-hour 'cooling down' period before they are operational. It should be noted, however, that a 17-hour battery may not provide enough service time for a two-shift operation if substantial overtime is involved.

Either charging method, or a combination of the two, is possible, depending on the system design and requirements. In addition to these automatic charging methods, some manufacturers provide secondary charging systems for situations where batteries fail. This system adds weight to the AGV, but if the battery is dead and the AGV is some distance from a charging station, power may be provided by a 480V ac extension.

Drive unit

The main components of a typical drive unit are the motor speed controller and the drive mechanisms. The carrier drive commands

Fig. 3.5   Drive unit

are generated either through the microcomputer or at the hand control unit. The output of the microcomputer in either case is used to energise the coil of the main power contactor to the drive motor speed controller. The drive speed and direction are separate variables that are also controlled by the microcomputer outputs. The drive motor (Fig. 3.5) may have an armature-mounted electromechanical disc brake that is spring applied and electrically disengaged, or it may have an electronic dynamic braking system to provide the desired deceleration.[4]

The drive motor speed controller is usually a pulse-width modulated four-quadrant servo drive unit. Some suppliers also employ internal current limiting in the event of a stalled motor. The emergency stop relay should be independent of the microcomputer and its status determined by all safety-related systems, such as bumpers and buttons. Many vehicles use Schabmuller motor-in-wheel units as the drives.

Steering

Vehicles are designed to manœuvre in three different ways: forward only, forward and reverse, and four-directional (Fig. 3.6). Forward motion requires one drive wheel and one steering system; forward and reverse motion requires an additional steering system; and four-directional motion requires at least two drive wheels and two steering systems.

Type of motion			Vehicle drive configuration	
Forward	Reverse	Crab		
✓	✓			Differential steering
✓				Single tricycle
✓	✓	✓		Dual tricycles

Fig. 3.6 Steering directions

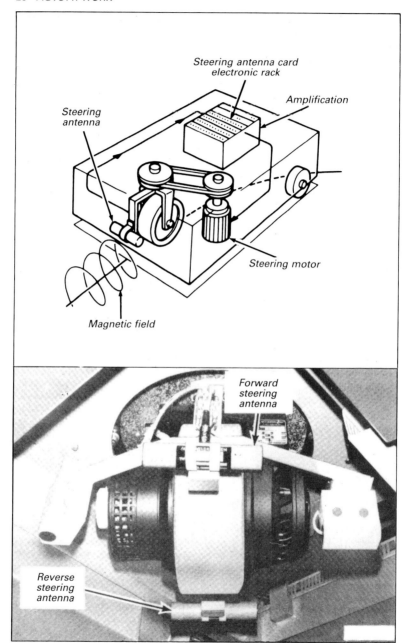

Fig. 3.7   Steering components

The major components of the steering system are: the steering antennae, the steering motors and their speed controller, the steering mechanical linkage and steering limit switches (Fig. 3.7).[4] In the manual mode the hand control unit is also part of the system and overrides the antenna circuitry.

Precision stop controller

AGVs must be able to stop with close locational accuracy at workstations and charging locations. A precision stop controller is used to accomplish this. At some point before an upcoming precision stop location, the vehicle will receive a precision stop command from the off-board control system or by code bars in the floor. As it approaches the stop point, the vehicle's metal detector (usually the precision stop is a long steel plate laid in the floor) is activated and the AGV slows to the end of the metal plate and stops. An optical guidepath vehicle would use an optical bar instead of a metal plate.

Depending on the type of vehicle, the stopping accuracy ranges from ±3 to ±0.010in. (approx. 7.5–0.025cm). Manual load/ unload operations can tolerate the ±3in. range, but greater accuracy is required for automatic transfer or for use with robots and other forms of automation.[2] For extra precision, 'V' notches can be cut into the floor for the vehicle wheels to nest into. When even greater precision is required, the vehicle may lower its work platform into tapered guide pins located in the floor (Fig. 3.8).

Fig. 3.8   Precision stop using tapered pins

On-board controller

Most manufacturing applications utilise 'smart' vehicles, i.e., in addition to a system of central controllers, each vehicle has its own microcomputer on board. (Conversely, a 'dumb' vehicle is one with no on-board processing capabilities.) The vehicle controller is similar to that of a robot and is used to monitor vehicle performance through encoder data to determine position and velocity. Discrete digital inputs monitor such functions as hand controls, activation of safety devices, battery condition, steering limits, brake release, running lights and drive controller status. The controller also provides outputs to activate and control such devices as the drive motor controller (speed and direction), charging contactors, safety devices and steering units.

In general, the microcomputer process instructions are received through communications from the off-board control system; the microcomputer also controls transmission of data to the control system. Some vehicle controllers allow the vehicle to be programmed to leave the guidepath, go to some pre-taught location, perform its task, and then back-track to the guidepath.

Communication unit

Instructions to the vehicle microcomputer are usually generated by the area (off-board) controller and then relayed to the vehicle. Likewise, the vehicle communicates its status back to the area controller.

The communication system may be either continuous or discrete. Continuous systems allow the vehicle and area controller to transmit and receive messages at any time using radio frequency (rf) methods or by use of communication wire within the guidepath. The discrete method provides for communication between the area controller and a particular vehicle only at predetermined positions (communication points). Communication in this case is by induction or optics.

The obvious disadvantages of discrete communication is that the area controller cannot communicate or receive vehicle status information until the vehicle reaches a communication point. Should a vehicle run into trouble between communication points, it could not inform the controller of its problem. However, even with this limitation, most systems use discrete communication methods. The chance of problems arising between stations is remote, and it is questionable if it is worth the added expense for the 'continuous' capability. Also, if rf communication is used, it can be distorted or disrupted by rf noise interference caused by large motors, and by welding and other industrial processes. (Chapter Six discusses in detail the various communication methods and their respective advantages and disadvantages.)

Safety

Safety systems may be divided into three specific categories: vehicle-to-vehicle, vehicle-to-object, and vehicle-to-people. Each of these systems is designed either to stop AGV motion or to communicate the next action of the AGV to personnel in the area. Manufacturers use various combinations of these systems to ensure the utmost safety of their AGV systems.

Vehicle-to-vehicle systems are used to maintain a minimum spacing between vehicles for collision avoidance (blocking). Blocking can be accomplished with photocells mounted on the AGV's leading edge and reflective material on the trailing edge. With such equipment, advancing vehicles are aware of others on the guidepath ahead. However, this system would not be sufficient

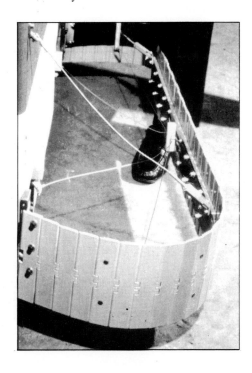

Fig. 3.9 Safety bumpers

for bidirectional carriers, since it is only effective in one direction. One solution is to use an ultrasonic or optic multifunction transceiver (transmits and receives) on the AGV's leading and trailing edges. The leading edge device is always in the receive mode, whereas the trailing edge always transmits.

When two AGVs are travelling towards each other (either head-on or into a guidepath intersection), the transceiver system does not prevent collisions. To do so, it is necessary to provide the area controller with a zone-block software program, or use a vehicle-to-object safety system. The off-board controller generally segments the guidepath into zones and allows only one vehicle at a time to enter a zone as it blocks (prevents) other vehicles from entering.

Vehicle-to-object safeguards are designed to protect both the vehicle and any object in the AGV's path. The devices most commonly used are bumpers (Fig. 3.9). Toe bars (rubber strips around the AGV about one inch off the floor, which, when compressed, stop the vehicle motion), limit switches, photocells, or proximity sensors, are other forms of safety device that can stop the vehicle (Fig. 3.10). The vehicle usually remains disabled for 3–6s after the stop signal clears (removing the object clears the signal), and then normal operation resumes. Often, the vehicle tooling has unique safety systems, especially if portions of the tooling details are motorised. These safeguards often require manual intervention.

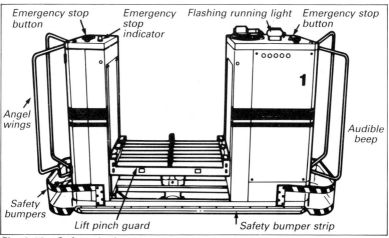

Fig. 3.10 Safety devices

Vehicle-to-people safety systems are designed both to warn and protect people. Generally vehicles have warning lights, buzzers or tones which flash or sound to indicate automatic mode, emergencies or faults. Vehicles are now being equipped with indicators and stop lights which inform personnel of a vehicle's intent at an intersection. Also, each vehicle is usually equipped with an emergency stop button.

Some vehicles are capable of travelling at speeds greater than 15ft/s (approx. 4.5m/s), but the maximum speed allowable should be 3.25ft/s (approx. 1m/s) to avoid overtaking pedestrian traffic and having to shut down.

Guidepath and guidance systems

Generally, most AGVs need a guidepath to follow. (Some vehicles are able to leave the guidepath for short distances and return to it, but these are still limited in application.) The guidepath techniques used are known as *passive* or *active tracking*. Passive tracking depends on either optical or metal detection principles, whereas active tracking involves inductive principles.

Passive tracking

The optical method may simply involve a light-sensitive photocell mounted on the vehicle which follows a tape on the floor. It depends on a contrasting floor surface so that variation in the

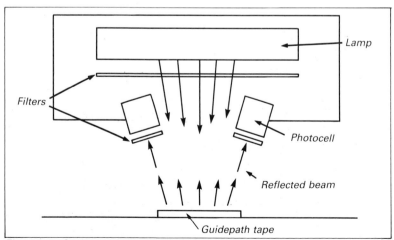

Fig. 3.11   Optical guidance techniques

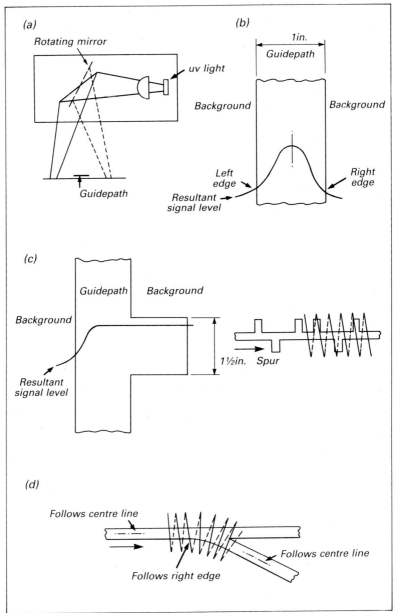

Fig. 3.12   Litton's optical guidance technique: (a) scanning sensor, (b) bell curve obtained from guidepath, (c) resultant signal obtanied from spur, and (d) following edge at branch

reflected light that is sensed by the photocell can detect when the vehicle begins to stray from the guidepath (Fig. 3.11). This signal is used to steer the vehicle back onto the guidepath. If the guidepath tape becomes dirty, faded or damaged, or if the ambient light distorts the light levels sensed, the vehicle may stray from the guidepath. (Most vehicles are designed to shut off if they do so.)

A variation of the optical method is Litton's patented optical system. It is based on bonding fluorescent particles to the floor surface and stimulating these particles with ultraviolet light causing them to emit a generated light. It is important to note that this is a generated light and not a reflected light and that the light spectrum generated is not found in ambient conditions. In the sensing head, an oscillating mirror scans the guidepath and reflects the generated light into a photoreceptor which in turn relays the signals to a microprocessor (Fig. 3.12a). The microprocessor interprets the light intensity as darkest on either side of the chemical strip and brightest in the centre. This shapes a mathematical bell curve representation of contrast values (Fig. 3.12b). The microprocessor averages these readings and thereby determines the centre line of brightness.

In order to identify 'landmarks' along the guidepath, such as branch identities or addresses at workstations, the Litton guidepath utilises short perpendicular spurs of the same chemical material at the appropriate points. The scanning sensor recognises these spurs by the absence of the normal bell shape. It senses a straight line of brightness to one side of the guidepath or the other (Fig. 3.12c). Depending on which side of the guidepath the spur is on, it represents a binary one or zero. The vehicle reads the binary sequence and interprets the code. When the vehicle reads a branch identity code, it determines (based on its destination) whether to proceed straight ahead on the guidepath or take the branching guidepath. It determines the correct edge of the desired path (right or left) and tracks that edge rather than the centre line. After a predetermined distance, the system reverts to following the centre line (Fig. 3.12d).

The other passive tracking technique involves vehicles with metal-detecting sensors following a stainless-steel ribbon. The Transcar patented guidance system consists of two sensor packs each containing five sensors and located at each end of the AGV. The three central sensors allow the vehicle to centre itself on the guide tape. The two remaining sensors assist the vehicle in traversing curves. The sensors locate the presence of the guide tape and transmit this information to the on-board microprocessor. The guide tape can be used on most floor surfaces and may also be installed on top of sub-floors, but must be installed beneath floor coverings such as tile, wood and carpet. The stainless-steel tape is resistant to solvents, cleaning agents and corrosion, and is virtually maintenance-free. The tape network can be easily modified and short breaks in the tape do not affect the guidance system.

Active tracking

Active tracking involves the use of a guidewire, and it is the most commonly used technique in industry. A low-voltage, low-current, low-frequency ac signal is conducted through a wire buried in a slot in the floor. A small electromagnetic field is radiated from the wire and two inductive-type sensors on the vehicle are used as the guidance detectors (Fig. 3.13). The signal magnitudes of the two sensors are compared, and as long as they are equal, the vehicle is centred on the guidepath. If the vehicle begins to stray, the signal magnitudes sensed are no longer equal, and the signal difference is then used to steer the vehicle back on the guidepath.

Floor and system controls

The controller is the brains of the whole system, tying the vehicle and guidepath together and integrating the system. Not only does

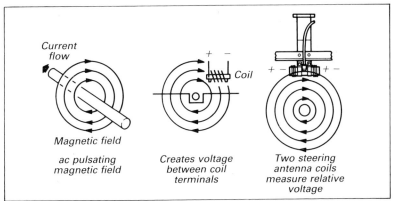

Fig. 3.13   Wire guidepath method of guidance

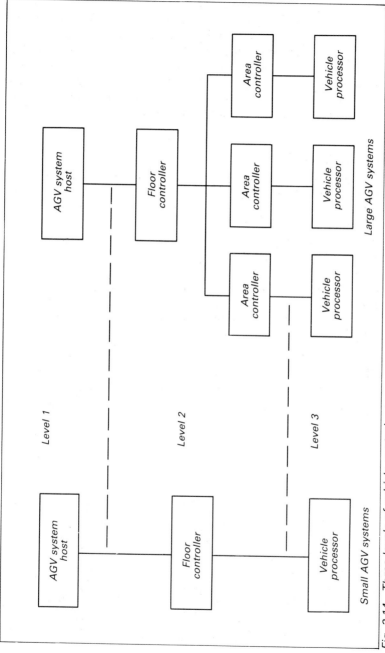

Fig. 3.14 Three levels of vehicle control

it control the AGV system, but it also integrates it with the flexible manufacturing and/or automatic assembly facility providing all the material handling. The AGV system itself will usually contain three levels of control architecture: vehicle control system, floor control unit, and vehicle on-board processor (Fig. 3.14). The following description of the functions and tasks performed by each level is general in nature and may vary from vendor to vendor.

Vehicle control system

The top level of the vehicle control system often communicates with, and is under the control of, the facility's host computer. This system control level is often referred to as the AGV controller or as the main-level computer. Most of the decision making takes place at this level as it oversees the system operation. As the knowledge centre of the system, it provides many services, including:

- Monitoring floor equipment status.
- Reporting inventory levels and vehicle utilisation.
- Supervising overall vehicle traffic.
- Tracking loads.
- Assigning destinations.
- Providing workstation definitions such as type, height, and lane selection.

The vehicle control system stores in memory exact vehicle locations at all times and provides network access. For integration into manufacturing environments, the vehicle controller needs to communicate information such as vehicle location and type of load to the facility's host computer. The final task for this control level is to act as the interface to allow users to generate reports, change product data, or make on-line system queries.

Floor control unit

This level is also referred to as the data concentrator and acts as the 'traffic manager', communicating directly with the vehicles and providing them with formatted, detailed commands. It, in essence, processes the communication between the central controller and the vehicles. Its functions or tasks are as follows:

- Provides lane selection based on such factors as style restrictions and work content.

- Makes carrier selection based on the closest available vehicle that is of the appropriate type.
- Sends information to the vehicle such as exact destination, build time, lift/lower heights.
- Provides system block and path selection for certain conditions, such as high priority moves, sequencing requirements, or failed guidepaths.
- Generates required guidepath frequencies.
- Provides collision avoidance.
- Controls factory-floor equipment (as designed into the system), collecting all floor inputs/outputs, such as AS/RS, conveyors, and push-button panels.

Vehicle processor

Generally the vehicle processor knows the vehicle location, can interpret commands received from the floor control unit, and can monitor the on-board safety devices. There are two basic types of vehicle processor: the intelligent type (automatic) and the non-intelligent type (semi-automatic). The non-intelligent type is not able to make decisions and requires such information as start, acceleration/deceleration commands, and external control to direct the vehicle to its final destination. This is usually accomplished by turning the guidepath on and off at decision points.

An intelligent or automatic vehicle contains a microprocessor which gives it many capabilities not exhibited by the non-intelligent type. Some of these extra on-board vehicle capabilities are as follows:

- Blocking between vehicles.
- Automatic routing permitting vehicles to find their own path to the final destination.
- Controlling speeds, accelerations, and decelerations.
- Interfacing with other types of equipment.
- Controlling the vehicle platform, such as raising/lowering a work platform or activating a load/unload mechanism.
- Releasing a vehicle from a workstation at a prescribed time.
- Uploading time spent at a workstation if the vehicle is released manually (this information is then used to select lanes and monitor throughput).
- Displaying job information to worker eliminating lost manifests.

- Providing built-in diagnostics to help reduce troubleshooting and repair times.

Finally, since the on-board vehicle processor has all these capabilities, some systems have the ability to run in a degraded mode should the floor control unit or the central control computer fail.

In summary:

AGV systems are made up of similar components. However, components from different vendors cannot be mixed within one system. The vehicles consist of the frame, batteries, on-board charging unit, electrical system, drive unit, steering, precision stop unit, on-board controller, communication unit, and safety system.

The guidepath techniques used are passive (optical, chemical, or metal) or active (induction) tracking. The optical guidance techniques used consist of paint and adhesive strips or tape used on a contrasting floor surface. The chemical technique involves painting a chemical strip containing fluorescent material that reflects ultraviolet light for the optical sensors to follow. Active tracking involves the use of a guidewire, and is the most commonly used.

AGV systems usually contain three levels in the control system. These are the vehicle control system, floor control unit, and vehicle processor. The vehicle control system is the top-level system and communicator with the facility's host computer. The floor control unit is considered the data concentrator, acting as the traffic manager for the vehicles. The vehicle processor may be either the intelligent or non-intelligent type and receives its commands from the floor control unit.

Chapter Four

Vehicle types

In the first chapter, the three major types of vehicle and various types of control systems used in AGV systems were briefly discussed. This chapter expands on that, and is intended to help managers and engineers to be able to specify the type of vehicles and controller needed for their facility. However, it should be borne in mind that although much detailed information is presented, it is not exhaustive as many vendors will design and build entire AGV systems to individual customer's specifications, including specialised vehicles and control systems.

Each type of major vehicle design has features that facilitate its use in a particular situation or application. It is, therefore, important to know the advantages and capabilities as well as the disadvantages and limitations of each type of vehicle. It is also possible to design an AGV system using different types of vehicle working together to perform the desired tasks. However, it is important to remember that different vendors' system components cannot be intermixed.

Unit load carriers

Unit load carriers are designed to carry individual loads on the vehicle's deck. The vehicles are usually rated in terms of deck-load capacity, which can range from less than 1000 to more than 20,000lb (approx. 450–9070kg). (Some may be as much as 150,000lb (approx. 68,040kg).) Vehicle payload catgories can be classified as light, medium, and heavy (Table 4.1).

The typical rating of commercially available unit load carriers is

Table 4.1   Unit load carrier payload categories

Category	Weight capacity (lb)	Application
Light	0–1000	Electronic industry and small part assembly
Medium	1000–4000	Flexible manufacturing and assembly
Heavy	4000–20,000	Machine tool industry

between 1000 and 4000lb (approx. 450–1810kg). Larger rated load capacity vehicles are specially designed and built for specific customer needs. The economics of large size vehicles are usually harder to justify.

Besides the load weight consideration, the load size is also an important factor and may limit the use of an AGV system. While the typical payload range is 20–20,000lb (approx. 9–9070kg) the size limitation is from 14×20×6in. to 6×16×6ft (approx. 36×51×15cm to 1.8×4.8×1.8m). The latter is about the size of most gondolas/containers or loaded pallets. The smaller size is suitable for small cartons or tote trays.

Unit load carriers can also be made for use as tugger vehicles and tow trailers; however, they usually do not function as well and cannot pull as much – the maximum draw-bar pull for a unit load carrier is between 160 and 200lb (approx. 73–91kg). The major advantages of unit load carriers over tugger systems are that they require less operation space, permit use of narrower aisles, and have a smaller turning radius (8ft (approx. 2.4m) intersections). Thus when unit load carriers are used as tuggers, this advantage is lost and the draw-bar pull capacity is much lower. A unit load carrier is basically designed to carry a single (or multiple) load on board its deck, whereas a tugger vehicle is designed to pull a trailer train, not vice versa.

Work platforms

The deck or work platform of a unit load carrier can be designed to do many tasks. Automatic load/unload capabilities should be considered for material-handling operations, such as delivering stock to manufacturing departments and CNC machines, or moving finished products.

Fig. 4.1 Powered roller conveyor deck

Powered conveyor. The deck can consist of a powered roller (Fig. 4.1) or chain conveyor. The vehicle positions itself alongside the stationary stand (a passive unit), such as an unpowered roller conveyor, and the on-board controller commences its unloading operation. Thereafter the vehicle is free for its next assignment.

Slave drive stand. This is similar to the powered conveyor deck, except that the stationary stand is also powered. The stand and vehicle deck conveyors are coupled together, and may be operated together or the stand can be the powered unit to conserve the vehicle's batteries. However, in this case, the floor controller, not the vehicle controller, needs to be in command.

Lift/lower deck. In this design, the deck of the vehicle can lift or lower its load upon command. The vehicle lifts its load and drives into a fixed unpowered stand designed to receive and hold the load. When in position, the vehicle on-board controller lowers the deck, depositing the load on the stand and freeing the vehicle for another assignment (Fig. 4.2). By reversing the process, the vehicle can also pick up a load.

Fig. 4.2   Raise/lower deck

Shuttle mechanism. This type of load/unload uses a vehicle with a non-powered roller conveyor or mechanical slides. The stand has a shuttle mechanism that accomplishes the loading and unloading. This requires a more expensive stand but a less sophisticated vehicle, thus reducing costs. Again the floor controller, instead of the vehicle controller, is in charge. If this level of control fails, the vehicles will not be able to continue to operate in a degraded mode, whereas they can if another transfer scheme is used.

Manual pick-up or deposit. It is always possible to use manual labour to load and unload the vehicle. The major problem is if a worker is not immediately available there will be a corresponding delay, causing the vehicle to be idle. This will produce inefficiencies and can disrupt throughput if there are insufficient vehicles to take up the slack. The temptation may be to use the vehicle as a buffer or storage device – they are much too expensive to be used as such. Manual load/unload should be considered only as a last resort.

Applications
The previous description of unit load carriers and their load/unload techniques mainly applies to material distribution. Another use of unit load carriers that is gaining much attention is the replacing of conveyor systems with vehicles in manufacturing.

Typical unit load carrier applications are outlined below.

CNC machining centre. For CNC machining centres, the unit load carriers can be designed to work in conjunction with CNC machines, delivering or picking up tooling, fixtures and parts. The system controller can coordinate the vehicle's load with the CNC machine's program so the proper tool, fixture or parts are being handled. This can greatly enhance the efficiency of the machining centre. Since human intervention is not needed, delays can be avoided. The machines can be kept running more often, even during off-shifts and break periods, thus improving a facility's throughput.

Flexible assembly. Another increasing use is in assembly operations, especially in the automobile industry. Here, a body, engine, or other component is assigned to a vehicle (unit load carrier), instead of being placed on a monorail, Cartrac, or other conveyor system. The vehicle then transports the components to an assembly area where an assembly team has the responsibility for a complete unit. This replaces an individual installing only one

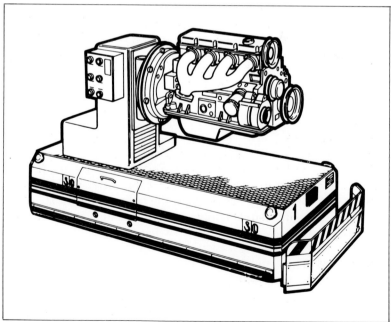

Fig. 4.3   Raise/lower deck for engine assembly

component or part. The advantages are numerous. The vehicle work platform can be designed to lift/lower, rotate, and tilt to permit better access to work areas (Fig. 4.3). Also, this allows for an asynchronous assembly process. The workers are able to work at their own pace, taking time to ensure a quality product. The team-building concept also tends to promote competition between working teams to build a better product in less time. The component can also remain with the vehicle through test cells and, if necessary, repair stations. The AGV system can resequence subassemblies later as needed, which would be difficult to accomplish with other types of conveying systems.

Light-load transporters. These are similar to other unit load carriers, except that they are designed to carry light loads and are smaller in size. The major applications will be in offices to pick up and deliver mail, messages, and light packages. In hospitals, light-load transporters are used to transport linens, surgical supplies and food. They are also used in electronic and other light assembly operations, including clean rooms.

Driverless tractors/trains (tuggers)

As previously discussed in Chapter One, the main application of driverless trains (tugger and several trailers) is for heavy material flow between a few destination points. The distances travelled between destination points should be at least 500ft (approx. 150m). This usually limits the application to warehousing environments which require material movement from shipping docks to the warehouse and from the warehouse to the manufacturing area. At the manufacturing area, the material is off-loaded and distributed manually by a conveyor, or by an AGV system using vehicles such as unit load carriers.

Size considerations

Most commercially available tuggers are rated at between 160 and 1000lb (approx. 73–454kg) of draw-bar pull. It is commonly assumed that the rolling resistance is approximately 2% of the rolling load. Thus, the corresponding rolling load to a draw-bar pull of 160lb would be 8000lb (approx. 3629kg) and to a draw-bar pull of 1000lb would be 50,000lb (approx. 22680kg). The weight of the trailers and load combined should be between 8000 and 50,000lb maximum, depending on the size of the tugger selected.

The number of trailers forming the train typically ranges from two to five.

The 2% rolling resistance is based on a smooth and level concrete floor. For example, three 5000lb (2268kg) capacity trailers require 300lb (136kg) draw-bar pull (3 × 5000 × 0.02 = 300). It is also necessary to consider static draw-bar pull – the pull required to start the load rolling. Other factors that can influence the rating are the type and condition of the floor, the slope of any ramps encountered, and the braking forces (especially going down ramps). The vendor will provide the necessary calculations to account for all these factors when sizing a tugger.

Trailers

The trailers can be any type, from simple castor-wheeled units to true-tracking units. The trailers are an important consideration in designing the AGV system, as the type and number of trailers will determine turning radius. This in turn will determine aisle and intersection requirements. Fig. 4.4 illustrates some of the types of trailers available.

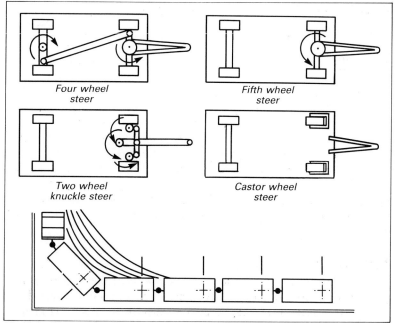

Four wheel steer

Fifth wheel steer

Two wheel knuckle steer

Castor wheel steer

Fig. 4.4　Types of trailer available

Fig. 4.5   Bottom view of a true-tracking trailer

The castor-wheel type trailer is the simplest and least expensive. However, it will not track the trailer in front while turning, and thus requires the largest turning radius of all types of trailer. This requires much larger intersections and aisle widths – the intersecting aisle widths required may be as much as 12ft (approx. 3.7m). However, the expense of the extra floor-space required can easily offset the savings experienced.

The true-tracking trailers are designed with a special steering linkage. This ensures that each trailer tracks or follows the path of the trailer in front of it (Fig. 4.5). These trailers are much more expensive, but only require 8ft (approx. 2.5m) intersecting aisles. Besides expense, another disadvantage is that they do not handle well if they have to be moved manually. Other trailer designs, such as fifth-wheel or front-wheel knuckle steering, provide benefits (aisle width requirements and cost) that fall between these two extremes.

Trailer decks

The trailer deck may be just a flat surface onto which gondolas/containers or pallets can be manually loaded or unloaded. Often AGV system design calls for the train to reach its destination and wait for a manually operated fork-truck to load/unload the trailers. For improved system efficiency, the trailers can be equipped with roller/chain conveyors, shuttle mechanisms, tilt bed, or lift/lower platforms to transfer the loads. Also, the stationary load transfer device could be the powered unit, and the trailer platform passive, such as non-powered rollers. System efficiency is, however, only gained with a significant increase in the cost of the trailers.

Another method of increasing AGV system efficiency is to use an open instead of closed system. A closed system is one in which the trailers are permanently attached to the tugger during normal operation. If the trailers are coupled or uncoupled, picking up or depositing them at various destinations, the system is referred to as an open system. The coupling/uncoupling may be either automatic or manual. For automatic coupling, the tugger is reversed, and an electromagnetic drop pin accomplishes the actual coupling. To uncouple a trailer at a destination point, the electromagnetic pin simply rises. The automatic coupling, although expensive, can possibly be justified by the elimination of operators to pull pins, plus the associated delays in waiting for an operator.

Manual operation

Most tuggers are designed such that manual operation is also possible. This means that an operator can take over the controls of the train and leave the guidepath to reach destinations not on the guidepath. However, when this occurs, the AGV control system loses track of the tugger and trailers. Thus, if a trailer is uncoupled, the control system would have no record of its whereabouts – the controller has to be given the new status when the train is returned to the guidepath.

Fork-style carriers

Pallet trucks

This type of vehicle is much more popular in Europe than in the USA because of the lack of standardisation in terms of size and construction of US pallets. Also, US pallets usually have bottom boards which sometimes make it difficult to insert or remove the forks from a lightly loaded pallet. European pallets ('Europallets') are standardised at 800×1200mm. They do not contain bottom boards, and all have the same construction.

The original pallet trucks were designed to lift the pallet 4–8in. (approx. 10–20cm) off the floor, travel to the programmed destination point, stop and lower the pallet to the floor, back out and return to the staging area. One of the major limitations was that an operator was required at the staging area to drive the vehicle (usually by a tiller steering device) off the guidepath to pick up another pallet. After engaging a pallet and lifting slightly, the operator needed to return the vehicle to the guidepath and program its next destination. The system depended on human intervention, which causes inefficiency. Another problem area is that the tines or forks had wheels near their extreme end. These wheels tended to snag the bottom boards of the pallet and, if the pallets were not heavily loaded, to drag them. The advantage of this type of vehicle was that it could lift off the floor without special load/unload devices. The disadvantage was that it was limited to depositing the pallet back on the floor and could not reach a conveyor or rack.

It is common for pallet trucks to have long wheeled tines up to 100in. (254cm) long, capable of handling two pallets at a time (Fig. 4.6). If the trucks have sufficient load capacity, it is also possible to have the pallets stacked two-high for a total of four at a time. Since the fork lift height is only 4–8in., stability is usually not a major problem. However, aisle requirements may limit their use; such requirements, especially intersection dimensions, are relative to the vehicle length including the forks. The total length for a vehicle with 100in.-long (254cm) forks will be considerable and will require large turning areas.

The latest pallet trucks now feature automatic pick-up at the staging areas, eliminating the need for human operators. Some can even leave the guidepath to pick up or deposit a pallet. Whereas the first pallet trucks were limited to floor-to-floor load transportation, the current type are designed to raise their loads to heights of about 40in. (approx.102cm). This now gives the pallet truck the capability of depositing on conveyors or racks, while still having the floor pick-up or deposit capability. The vehicles may still be operated manually when required, and have load capacities ranging from 1000 to 6000lb (approx. 454–2722kg).

The most suitable application for pallet trucks is for moving pallets or skids in a moderate material-flow density situation. Also, the distance should be moderate to long (over 300ft (approx. 91m)), with a relatively large number of pick-up and deposit stations. Fully automated pallet trucks provide for more

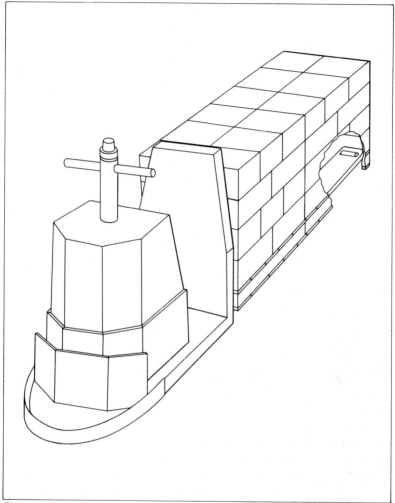

Fig. 4.6   Pallet truck with long tines and two pallets

throughput than that offered by unit load carriers, and can handle
loads (pallets and skids) at floor level. However, all loads must
have open access under the load platform to allow entrance of the
forks, and the vehicles must travel more slowly due to the inherent
load-carrying method. Also, when moving lightly loaded pallets
with bottom boards, the wheeled forks tend to catch on the boards
when the vehicle is reversing out after depositing the load.

High-lift trucks

Several names are given to this type of vehicle: 'automated industrial trucks', 'high-lift unit load trucks', 'automated fork-trucks', or 'high-lift pallet trucks'. This type of vehicle has very similar characteristics to a pallet truck, except the lift height is greatly extended to as much as 20ft (approx. 6.1m). In many cases, they also offer greater manœuvrability. But as with pallet trucks, high-lift trucks are able to pick up loads at floor level.

For stability, many of these vehicles are built with straddle arms or outriggers (Fig. 4.7). Because of the stability offered by the straddle arms, the loads do not have to be carried at the 4–8in. height restriction as with pallet trucks – the weight of load is transferred to the straddle arms; therefore the tines or forks do not need wheels at their ends. This type of vehicle can readily be used with pallets with bottom boards. For vehicles with a maximum required lift height of 6–8ft (approx. 1.8–2.4m), the masts are of

Fig. 4.7   High-lift truck with straddle arms

*Fig. 4.8 Counterbalanced
side-load reach truck*

the fixed type, but for vehicles with greater lifting ability 8–20ft
(approx. 2.4–6.1m), the masts are of the telescopic type. This
allows the vehicles to travel through areas that have low ceilings
and also through doorways. The maximum load for this type of
vehicle is about 6000lb (approx. 2720kg).

Other variations in design include counterbalanced trucks that
eliminate the need for straddle arms. This reduces the vehicle
width by 16–20in. (approx. 40–50cm), but the counterbalancing
adds to the overall vehicle length. Also, the reach is limited since
the stability is not as great as that obtained with straddle arms.

Yet another variation is the counterbalanced reach truck. This
design provides for forks that extend to pick up a load and then
retract over the truck body before the vehicle moves. This acts
more like a unit load carrier in terms of vehicle stability, and also
provides a vehicle of shorter length. Again, because of stability
problems this type of vehicle has limited reach.

Fig. 4.9   Side-load truck lifting racks

The final variation is the side-load vehicle; Figs. 4.8 and 4.9 show a combination reach and side-load truck.

In summary:

Unit load carriers are designed to carry individual work-loads on the deck. The deck serves as a work platform and automatic load/unload capabilities should be considered for material-handling operations, such as delivering stock to manufacturing or moving finished products. Unit load carriers are rated according to deck-load capacity and are classified as light, medium or heavy.

Tractors or tuggers are used for heavy material flow over long distances with few stops. Common applications are material movement in warehouses. The type of trailer used will determine the required turning radius and plays a major part in designing the system. The trailer decks can be equipped with transfer mechanisms to improve efficiency.

Pallet trucks and high-lift vehicles are used for moderate material flow over moderate to long distances with a large number of stops. A major feature of these vehicles is that they can pick up and deposit loads (mostly pallets or skids) at floor level without extra fixturing. Pallet trucks are limited to lift heights of about 40in. (approx. 102cm), while high-lift vehicles can reach heights of 20ft (approx. 6.1m).

Chapter Five

Control considerations

The vast improvements experienced in the area of AGV controls have provided for more sophisticated material-handling systems in manufacturing. These advancements are included in both the system control and the basic vehicle control. The advent of powerful, yet relatively inexpensive, micro-computers has made this feasible.

Control objectives

The overall objective of a control system should be to provide reliable stand-alone material handling and tracking, and it should work jointly with the facility's host computer for material-handling management. The material-handling capability should provide for total plant inventory, storage, transportation, and real-time tracking control. The materials involved include raw materials, purchased components, tooling, and other items used in manufacturing. Not to be overlooked, however, are facility support materials, such as maintenance parts, cleaning supplies, refuse and scrap, and even mail.

The function of a control system is two-fold: information control (know what we have, how much we have, and where it is at all times) and physical control (what we want, where we want it, when we want it). These should be integrated when material is in storage, transit, and in process. The control system consists of the computer hardware and software, the procedures to make it operate and the personnel (both operators and maintenance personnel) required for operations. Without proper planning and provision for each of these areas, serious problems will result.

Control philosophies

Two major control philosophies exist: central processing and distributed processing. In central processing schemes, all essential functions for the facility material-handling AGV system (AS/RS) are performed by one central processor which controls all the various devices (Fig. 5.1). In distributed processing, processing is accomplished at the lowest possible level (Fig. 5.2). This permits each individual system to perform much of the processing task, thus being able to function as a stand-alone unit.[5]

The advantages of the central processing scheme are that it requires less equipment and personnel, it is easier to 'back up' the system, and all information is centrally located. The advantages of the distributed processing scheme are that it provides stand-alone processing and is faster. This helps ensure that the entire system will not go 'down' even though one part fails. It also makes it easier to expand the system without a complete system redesign;

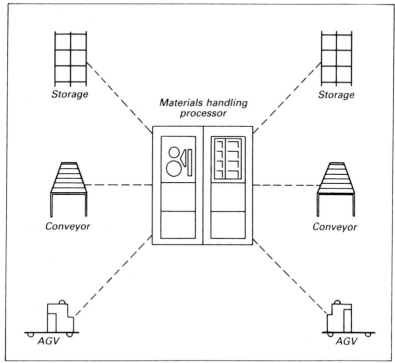

Fig. 5.1 Central processing scheme

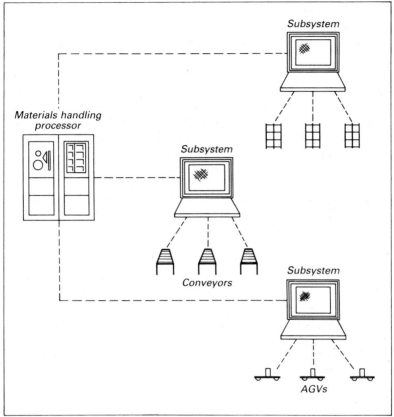

Fig. 5.2 Distributed processing scheme

it makes testing and debugging easier since this is accomplished on a subunit basis; and since processing is accomplished at the lowest level it helps prevent delay in time-sensitive operations.

Since the control system is the brains of the entire AGV system, it is imperative that much thought is given to its specification. The AGV system must be able to interface with the rest of the facility, for example, robots, AS/RS, conveyors, and the facility's host computer. It is important to specify exactly what the AGV vendor is responsible for in terms of interfacing with the rest of the facility, the type of networking, communications and information necessary. It is also important to have long-range plans in mind so that the control system can be designed to accommodate implementation of other automation in the future.

Control specification considerations

Several questions need to be addressed before specifying the control system:[5]

- What is to be controlled? – Products, tooling, and fixtures.

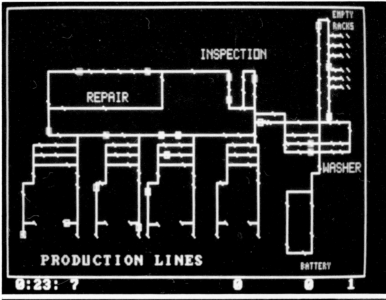

Fig. 5.3 Graphical display of status: (a) screen view and (b) overall view

- How much control is desired? – Real-time tracking; inventory update; charge material to employee on job.
- Where is it to be controlled? – In the process area; in the storage area; in transit.
- How is the control to be done? – Automatic; semi-automatic; manual.
- What is the required information flow speed?
- What degree of operation is required in a degraded mode, should the system controller fail?
- How flexible should the system be? – Program modifications by the supply only; menu driven by an operator.

A graphical system display should be considered when specifying the system controller. It provides an animated picture of the AGV system and is a key user-interface tool. Instead of having to review reams of paper for determining the system status, it will be displayed in graphical form as shown in Fig. 5.3. Information displayed includes:

- Vehicle location.
- Next destination.
- Whether vehicle is moving or is stationary.
- Malfunctioning vehicles.
- Battery status.

This data can provide performance information on the system, including areas creating bottlenecks, locating particular jobs in the system, and helping determine proper bank sizes.

Back-up considerations

Computer back-up capability is a vital consideration, especially for complex systems. The computers contain information about current AGV floor status, such as the vehicles in operation, vehicles in repair or being charged, vehicle locations, vehicle destinations, vehicle loads/material being transported, as well as status of interfacing components, such as robots, AS/RS, CNC machines and conveyors. If sufficient computer back-up is not available and the computer should 'crash', vital material-handling system control information, as well as material monitoring information, will be lost. This would cause great disruption to both the material-handling capability and to material records keeping.

Most AGV systems use redundant system architecture (Fig. 5.4), utilising an extra system computer that turns on automatic-

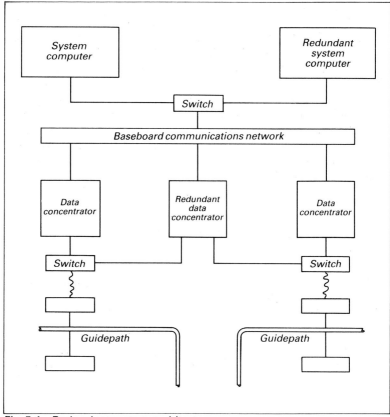

Fig. 5.4   Redundant system architecture

ally in the event of a system computer crash. This is not essential when using a distributed control system and smart vehicles. This type of architecture is expensive since purchase of nearly two complete system controls is necessary. Besides expense, a redundant system has another disadvantage in that the redundant computer must 'cold start' to regain system control when the main computer fails. If the redundant computer has not been used for a while, it may not perform as expected, and the user may end up with two system computers down and no AGV system. To overcome this problem, the back-up should be continually switched on with the primary computer. Another solution is to use the primary computer for the system control and to use the back-up for non-essential operations, such as report generation and graphical system display. If the primary computer fails, the back-up can readily be switched over to perform the system control. This method ensures that the back-up is always operational; it also permits the use of less powerful and expensive computers since the tasks are shared between the primary and back-up units.

An alternative is now being offered and is based on parallel processors being used to form the system computer, as shown in Fig. 5.5. Both processors work continuously, unlike redundant systems in which only one computer is being used at a time. In parallel processing, if either one of the computers fail, the other one acquires the failed computer's tasks in addition to its own.

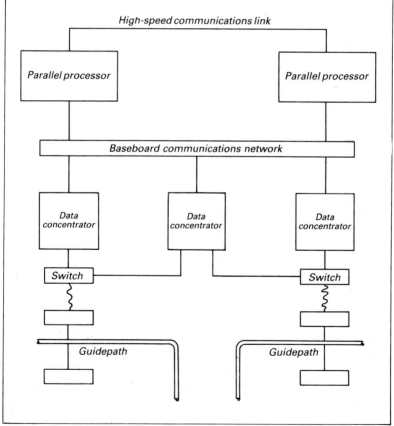

Fig. 5.5   Parallel computer architecture

This is achieved by having each computer continuously monitor the other and knowing exactly where the other computer is in its tasks. In the event of a computer failure, the remaining computer takes over both tasks, keeping the system operation at a reduced performance. This gives the parallel processing system a high degree of fault tolerance. However, experience has shown failings in error detection and data logging, inasmuch as realising which processor is in error and which is correct, and the length of time taken to log data both to the system disk and to other systems – with such a time period the processor may be busy and miss some data.

Software

The computer software is an intangible aspect of AGV systems and is often the weak link. To help eliminate some of the most common limitations in the control system, the software should be specified to provide:

- *Flexibility*. The software should allow the user to change minor aspects of the system operating parameters, such as routes and workstation cycle times, without requiring vendor participation. It should also be minor-fault tolerant.

- *User interaces*. A simple menu should be provided to allow the users to generate reports, change product data, and have on-line system queries.

- *Maintainability*. This will allow for in-house enhancements to accommodate major changes, such as changing a station from manual to automatic, or adding system interfaces such as another conveyor.

AGV controls

Some AGV systems use vehicles which have sophisticated microcomputers on-board and are known as 'smart or intelligent vehicles'. Other systems have minimal vehicle computing ability and use a central computer to process all functions. In such a system, the central computer determines the vehicle's location, its destination, and the proper route, and it directs the vehicle's path and velocity. This is accomplished by turning on and off the path at decision points or by commanding the vehicle to follow a particular frequency. All decision making is thus performed by the central computer. With smart vehicles the central computer dispatches the vehicle to the next location. Through its on-board microprocessor, the vehicle itself makes its own decision as to which path it takes.

In both cases, the central computer monitors the vehicle movements. Smart vehicles are able to carry out their functions under semi-automatic on-board control or by a back-up central control even if the main controller is not operating. In addition, smart vehicle controllers are able to start and stop the vehicle, avoid other AGV traffic (through blocking and anti-collision), communicate remotely with the central computer, control work platforms (such as load/unloading), and interface with other equipment (such as conveyors, AS/RS, and CNC machines).

Methods of programming/control

The simplest system uses manual programming to direct the vehicle to specific destinations (stations) and to dispatch the vehicle. These systems range from basic toggle switches, thumbwheel switches, or push-button numeric pads for programming the vehicle to go to a specific station, to more sophisticated key-pads which enable entry of multiple stops and priorities. The typical sequence of operations for a manual dispatching control would be as follows:

1. Operator loads the vehicle.
2. Operator inputs the destination and dispatches vehicles.
3. AGV control system routes the vehicle to its destination.
4. At the appropriate stop, the load is deposited.
5. The vehicle waits for further input from the operator.

The advantage of a manual system is that it is the least expensive and simplest of the available systems. The major disadvantage is that the system efficiency is dependent upon the operators. Operators need to load and unload in a timely manner, and likewise, if the operators must wait for vehicles, it can also produce worker inefficiency. Also, there is the possibility of dispatching errors. Finally, this type of system lacks tracking capability, and so the system controller cannot determine vehicle location whilst in transit.

The second level of sophistication in control systems is referred to as 'remote dispatch'. In such a system, operators interact with the local controller which in turn transmits information, such as destination, route, and automatic load/unload commands, to the vehicle. The typical sequence of operations is:

1. Dispatch to a workstation.
2. Automatic loading.
3. Vehicle given its destination and route, then dispatch.
4. Automatic unloading.
5. Released for next assignment.

This control system allows the vehicle to circulate on the guidepath looking for work. It also increases the system efficiency since it does not depend upon operators for loading/unloading and dispatching. However, these systems do not offer tracking capabilities.

The third level is still more complex and expensive and is referred to as the 'central computer controlled system'. In such systems, all vehicle transactions are monitored by the system central computer and are connected to the facility's host computer. This permits interfacing the AGV system with AS/RS, CNC machines, and process control equipment. It also allows for complete automatic material control. Operator errors are minimised since most commands are received from the host computer. When commands are entered manually, they are scanned for errors and only valid commands are accepted. Tracking is also possible with this level of sophistication, including colour graphics displaying the guidepaths, location and status of all the vehicles. This can be used to spot system bottlenecks quickly.

Other capabilities include interfacing with automatic doors to open and close them by means of signals from the computer. Also in the central computer controlled system, the vehicles can use freight elevators to carry loads between floors and can have control over the vehicles (for example, slow down the vehicle) while on ramps and in tunnels. Efficiency is greatly enhanced in this type of system control and a high degree of flexibility is permitted by information transfer into the facility production and inventory control, providing complete feedback on material status.

In summary:

The control system's overall objective should be to provide reliable stand-alone material handling and tracking, including both information control and physical control. There are two major control philosophies: central processing and distributed processing. Central processing performs all essential functions within one central processor, whereas distributed processing accomplishes each task within each individual system. Before control specifications can be made, the product level of control, area of control and method of control must be considered.

The computer software for an AGV system should provide flexibility, user interfaces and maintainability, and even be 'menu' driven. AGV controls can have minimal vehicle computing ability, requiring control from the central computer, or they can be smart vehicles carrying on-board microcomputers which allow the vehicle to make its own decisions. The methods of programming and controlling are manual dispatch, remote dispatch, and central computer control. Central computer control permits a high degree of flexibility and improves efficiency.

Chapter Six

Guidance and communications

An AGV system is totally dependent upon the guidance
system to guide the vehicles as they travel from a given
location to their next destination. There are several guidance
techniques commercially available but the most commonly used
are the active 'wire guidepath' or passive 'optical guidepath'
techniques. Each type has its own set of advantages and
disadvantages, and it is important that the user be aware of them
so the most suitable method may be selected.

Guidepath techniques

Passive techniques

Passive guidance techniques, already discussed in Chapter Three,
involve the use of chemical, paint, and adhesive strips or tape,
whereby the AGV focuses a beam of light on the reflective tape or
painted strip and tracks the path by measuring the amplitude of
reflected or stimulated light. Another passive method involves
vehicles with metal-detecting sensors following a stainless-steel
tape. The vehicles can be programmed to follow either the right
edge or left edge of the guidepath, and as other paths veer off
either to the left or right, the vehicle will follow the edge onto the
new path. Communication of commands and positional information to the vehicles may be accomplished by placing guidepath
codes along the guidepath. (This method is discussed in detail in
the communication section of this chapter.) Other data transfer
from the system controller is limited to either radio frequency or
optical methods.

The advantages of using optical guidepaths are that it is a very low cost method, easy to apply, will not damage the floors, and is easily and quickly modified. The disadvantages are that the guidepath is easily damaged, requires continual maintenance, does not tolerate dirt, and requires an rf or optical communication system, which is often unreliable (the guidepath cannot transfer data). These features make it particularly useful in offices (e.g. delivering mail), hospitals (e.g. delivering food and laundry), and in clean-room environments where slotting the floor would not be acceptable, or where a temporary system or path is necessary. Likewise, it is not usually suitable for harsh industrial environments, although the metal-tape method is more rugged than the optical methods.

Active techniques

By far the most commonly used method in industry is the wire guidepath. This method involves cutting a slot in the floor ⅛–¾in. (approx. 0.32–1.9cm) wide and ½–1½in. (approx. 1.27–3.81cm) deep into which one or more wires are placed and grouted or epoxyed in (Fig. 6.1).

Fig. 6.1 Installation of guidewire in floor slot

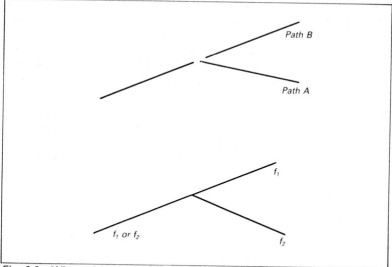

Fig. 6.2   Wire guidepath guidance techniques: (a) guidance by segments, and (b) guidance by assigned frequencies

There are two different wire guidepath techniques, one using either one wire in the slot operating at one frequency or with multiple overlaid frequencies, and the other using several wires in the slot each operating at a different frequency. The first method involves incremented lengths of guidewire discontinuous at decision points (Fig. 6.2a), whereby the system controller turns the various segments on and off to direct the vehicle into the correct path or for blocking. For AGV systems using dumb vehicles, the floor controller does all the routing control from its level. For systems using smart vehicles, which decide their own routing, the vehicles (when reaching a decision point) will communicate commands to the floor controller to turn on the appropriate guidewire segment. The floor controller will then turn the requested segment on, unless blocking is required.

With the multiple-wire method, a path is selected at decision points according to the assigned frequencies (Fig. 6.2b). The vehicle can be programmed or directed by the system controller at decision points to follow the appropriate frequency, and thus the vehicle is directed onto the desired path. For example, Volvo's guidance system uses up to five wires with the following frequencies: $f_0 = 1000\text{Hz}$, $f_1 = 1147\text{Hz}$, $f_2 = 1323\text{Hz}$, $f_3 = 1515\text{Hz}$, and $f_4 = 1730\text{Hz}$.

Just as perpendicular bars are used in optical guidepaths to provide certain instructions to vehicles, wire guidepath systems use magnets or metal plates embedded in the floor. Such instructions include activation of horns or other signals, indication of communication loop and command reception from controller, speed change, selection of appropriate path at decision points, and stops.

The control system can also communicate through radio telemetry on a narrow UHF band frequency, although this is often unreliable in industrial environments unless a dedicated frequency is used. However, most systems communicate by multiplexing digital data through the guidewire itself or through inductive loops embedded in the floor at various designated communication points throughout the system floor layout. When the vehicle passes over any of these communication points, the rf system is activated, transmitting over a short distance with the inductive loop (antenna) (Fig. 6.3). This results in a communication system which is much more reliable and hence requires less maintenance.

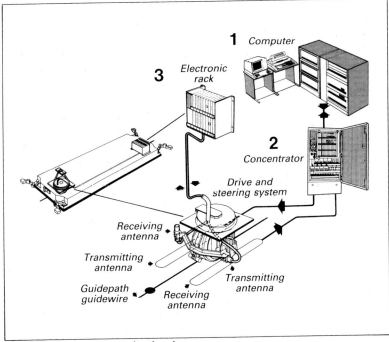

Fig. 6.3   Floor communication loops

The advantages of a wire guidepath are its reliability, low maintenance, and proven control system in industrial environments. However, wire guidepaths are more difficult to install and modify, since they usually require slotting or cutting of the floor. Also, they are difficult to repair if a wire is broken or damaged, and require approximately 10ft (3.05m) of clearance from arc welders and similar equipment which can cause interference with the communication wires.

Other guidepath techniques

The disadvantages associated with the use of wire guidepaths and optical guidepaths have prompted the development of other guidance techniques, such as deadreckoning, infrared, gyro, and laser-imaging pattern recognition. The advantages of these methods are that there is no need for floor cutting, and they are easily modified and thus highly flexible. However, as with all methods, guidance systems using these techniques exhibit some disadvantages: they are expensive; the communication is limited to rf or optical methods; and they are not nearly as accurate in terms of positioning. In addition, such guidance techniques remain unproven in industrial environments.

Deadreckoning. Some AGV suppliers are now offering off-wire guidance through the use of deadreckoning. By monitoring the number of revolutions and orientation of its wheels, the vehicle is able to trace a preprogrammed route to find a remote location, then retrace its path and return to the guidepath. This gives the system the reliability of wire-guidance techniques, and has the flexibility of quick system modification to cope with temporary work destination instructions.

Infrared. By strategically placing reflective targets at the end of aisles, the vehicle can navigate by 'homing-in' using an infrared beam. A potential problem is limited guidance system abilities, requiring basically a straight line or line-of-sight to the target. It is also difficult to work around obstacles, and should pedestrian and other traffic in the aisles interrupt the beam the vehicle would stop.

Gyro. A gyroscope on board the vehicle maintains a base reference as the vehicle travels through the facility. This consists of setting up the axis of a gyroscope parallel to the direction of motion of the vehicle. If the vehicle deviates from its path, an acceleration will occur perpendicular to the direction of motion which is detected by the gyroscope. By integrating twice, the displacement from the vehicle's path can be calculated. From this value and the programmed facility's routes, the vehicle is able to find its destination from any other location.[6]

Pattern recognition. With this type of system, the vehicle is 'taught' to recognise its position from its surroundings (pattern). It can 'find' its way to a destination by looking for certain areas or devices. This type of system also has a potential problem: if the pattern is changed, for example a machine moved or a bin of parts placed in the working area, the vehicle recognises the discrepancy and stops. It then requires human intervention to indicate that it is permissible to proceed.

Robot Defense Systems (RDS) has developed a sophisticated 3D laser imaging sensor, 'the OWL', based on a high-speed rastering infrared laser beam. An array of integer numbers ranging from 0 to 4095 is returned from the sensor for each 'pixel' in the array. The further a scanned object is from the sensor, the larger is the returned number. The sensor is capable of detecting objects up to 140ft (approx. 43m) away and can operate in either full daylight or in complete darkness. Coupled with LISP software, this sensor has the ability to enhance autonomous operations by providing detailed information about unknown environments. The 3D laser imaging software consists of several components; of primary interest is the real-time RDS '3D World Model Generation' module coded in LISP. This module is responsible for integrating data from sensors mounted on the vehicle, generating a 3D model of the local world, and maintaining this model as new information becomes available. This world model is based upon input received in real-time from the laser imaging system and is not dependent upon previously acquired digitised planning maps. The system allows for a near autonomous vehicle capable of self-navigation to travel through a cluttered natural environment.

Communication techniques

Irrespective of the guidance technique used, it is essential for the individual vehicle to be able to communicate with the system controller. The vehicle must be able to receive such commands as work assignment, destination, route, frequency, speed, blocking instructions, when to start and stop, and auxiliary equipment commands. Similarly, the vehicle must be able to transmit its status to the system controller by sending such information as vehicle identification, location, direction of travel, speed of travel, and battery status.

There are two classifications for AGV communication systems: continuous and discrete. Continuous indicates that the area controller can always communicate with any vehicle, whereas discrete means that the area controller can only communicate with a particular vehicle at certain times (usually determined by vehicle position). Such positions are commonly referred to as communication points.

Radio frequency communication is a widely used form of continuous communication. Each AGV is equipped with a transmit/receive antenna (Fig. 6.4), and the area controllers generally have a number of similar antennae strategically positioned throughout the facility. Each AGV may be on a different frequency, or an address polling algorithm may be used by the area controller allowing the same frequency for communication. In manufacturing applications, large motors or spot-welding processes in the vicinity of the AGV system can create rf noise which interferes with the communication broad-

Fig. 6.4   Transmitting and receiving antennae

casts. Some suppliers provide inductive communication systems whereby a second set of wires is layered in the floor with the guidepath wires or alternatively multiplex digital data is transmitted through the guidewire itself.

The majority of AGV system manufacturers prefer discrete communication methods, inductive and optical. Inductive communication systems utilise a set of wires buried beneath the floor along the guidepath in squares or rectangles to form communication points. Each communication point is assigned a unique address through the area controller. To communicate, vehicles either come to a stop with their communication antenna immediately above a communication loop, or while in motion over an elongated loop (elongated in the direction of travel). Also, the area controller may either have one loop for both transmitting and receiving or have separate side-by-side loops, one for transmitting and the other for receiving (Fig. 6.5). The latter is used to double

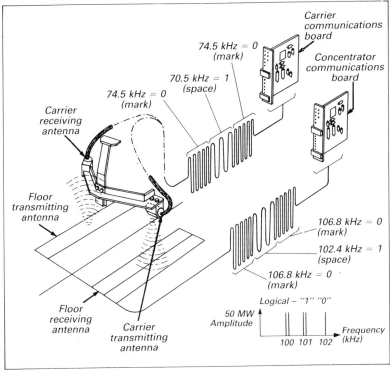

Fig. 6.5   Vehicle communicating at communication loop

the receiving loop for improved communication with the AGV (since the vehicle does not generally have as strong a transmitter as the area controller). The frequency range for communication is usually 70–100kHz.

The optical method involves stopping the AGV at set stations along the guidepath where information is passed to the vehicle using infrared light. Another type of optical communication is through the use of light emitting diodes (LEDs) such as those commonly found in pocket calculator displays. NEC Technologies has developed a system that uses LEDs located at communication points to track, position and guide a vehicle on a preprogrammed course. Positioning of the vehicle is performed by a detector on the vehicle that determines the angle of the light source in relation to the vehicle. The detector senses the centre of the light image and generates output signals that are converted into digital or

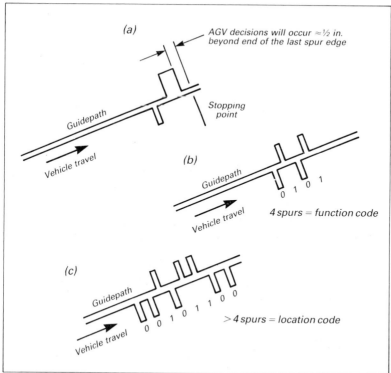

Fig. 6.6 Binary code bars in floor: (a) marker, (b) function code, and (c) location code

analogue outputs for directional information. Vehicle communication is accomplished through sequencing the LEDs at the communication points. This type of guidance can be used with inductive wire-guided systems – when a vehicle enters an area employing in-floor wire guidance or magnetic tape, it can operate on the existing guidance system without the need for any separate controller. This system is useful if a vehicle needs to leave the wire guidepath.

Both rf and optical communication techniques provide means of communicating commands and information between the mobile AGV and the fixed area or floor controller. Commands and information are continually being updated, as required by the devices served by the AGV system. A more limited form of communication, in which commands cannot be readily changed, is accomplished by placing guidepath codes along the guidepath. These codes are formed by adding short spurs perpendicular to the guidepath in a binary fashion (Fig. 6.6). The spurs provide binary codes which are detected and decoded by the vehicle. The codes are used to identify location points along the guidepath or to instruct the vehicle to carry out specific functions. Some possible functions include sounding a horn, disabling the proximity sensor to permit passage around fixed objects, identifying stops, and transmitting remote commands. The latter signals can be used to activate external devices, such as a door-opening device.

These guidepath codes are commonly used with optical guidepath techniques, although they can be used with wire guidepath systems. For these systems, magnetic foil tape is used to provide such functions as listed above. Again, the vehicle reads the codes and is preprogrammed to interpret the meaning.

Guidepath layout considerations

Considerable expertise is necessary to detail the layout for the guidepath. (Since the detailed engineering of AGV systems is not this book's purpose, the reader is referred to the reference list for further information.) AGV suppliers have the expertise and will detail the guidepath design for a particular facility to meet individual needs. However, there are general guidelines that should be considered to increase the system efficiency:

- The system should be designed so that the vehicles are kept busy and do not travel 'empty' or stand idle.

- To prevent excessive or needless travel, the layout should provide for alternative routes.
- Critical timing for the vehicle should be avoided by providing buffer zones for some material being delivered or removed.
- Pinch points should be avoided by providing at least 12in. (approx. 30cm) when vehicles pass each other or fixed objects.
- Battery charge areas should be located near the activity (excessive travel distances should be avoided when a charge is needed).
- One-way traffic on a guidewire is best with spurs for a vehicle to use where it is required to perform a task. This permits the main guidepath to remain open for other vehicles.
- Aisles with heavy pedestrian traffic should be avoided.
- The layout should be planned for extreme conditions (maximum production activity).
- Long dead-end spurs should be avoided if serviced by more than one vehicle.

In summary:

There are many guidepath techniques and communication methods available. Indeed, many AGV suppliers offer more than one type and even offer hybrid systems to meet customers' special needs. Typical guidepath techniques commercially available include optical, wire guidance (the most common), deadreckoning, infrared, gyro, and pattern recognition. Wire guidance has proven its reliability in harsh industrial environments, but requires slotting the floor which usually precludes it from use in the electronics industry, hospitals and offices. In such environments, the other guidance techniques are more suitable.

Communication methods include coding the guidepath to give the vehicle special commands at specific locations. However, this technique does not allow communication with the area controller. Most systems use radio frequency or optical methods of communication. These communication methods are designed to pass information back-and-forth between the AGV's microprocessor and the area controller.

Chapter Seven

Economic considerations

The goal of any industry is to remain competitive in the market-place while making a reasonable profit for its shareholders. For manufacturing industries, especially in light of foreign competition, this involves improving existing facilities or building new and better ones. Associated with these changes is the opportunity to investigate alternative and improved methods of material handling. AGV systems provide such an alternative.

A major problem associated with implementing a change is that AGV systems are relatively new and remain untested in many applications. Even though AGV systems may be utilised to optimise material-handling performance, certain parameters make it difficult to justify them economically. This chapter elaborates on some of the parameters that could be used for economic justification.

Economic factors

Several factors, such as direct investment costs (i.e. the AGV system), direct annual savings (i.e. labour and material), and direct annual operating costs (i.e. maintenance and utilities) are fairly obvious. However, there are many other less apparent factors to take into account when estimating the cost of an AGV system. It is often difficult to place a monetary value on these factors, but they do have a significant effect on the overall economic impact.

Installation. An AGV system can be installed more quickly and more economically than most other material-handling systems if it has been properly simulated and programmed. Otherwise, the debugging time may be considerable. They can also be installed in existing buildings with a minimum of interference to ongoing operations. However, if the existing floor is not suitable, it may be expensive preparing it.

System modification. Guidepaths can be easily modified or expanded following material movement changes or as the plant size increases, as long as it was planned for in the original system. AGV systems can be designed with large numbers of pick-up and delivery points, which can be easily modified. Also, system capacity can often be increased by adding vehicles as and when necessary.

Interfacing with other automation. AGV systems can be easily interfaced with other material-handling systems including conveyors, AS/RS, production lines, robots, and even such devices as doors and elevators. However, the I/O requirements can increase the cost of the system considerably.

Operation. AGV systems have reliable system capacity. If one vehicle breaks down, the entire system is not crippled because the vehicles are independent of each other (assuming that a 'crippled' vehicle is removed from the system and is not allowed to block a zone). A spare vehicle can keep the system at its rated capacity while the disabled vehicle is being repaired in the maintenance shop.

Inventory control. With an AGV system, inventory is reduced and all material is tracked by the computer control system. This allows for better performance scheduling, on-line interface to production and inventory control systems, and management information on workstation production. There is greater control over lead-time, cycle rates and work-in-progress inventory, which stabilises the production process and provides better line balance.

Environment. The installation of an AGV system improves the working environment in a plant. The system requires relatively little energy to operate and the vehicles are very quiet. Also, there are no obstructions in the aisles, which contributes to good housekeeping.

Reduced product damage. There is less product and plant equipment damage because the vehicles travel on a predetermined route and contain safety features that make it virtually impossible to collide with racks and other obstacles.

Operator accountability. An AGV system inherently transfers responsibility for quality to the production operators. The operators are allowed enough time to do the job right the first time, making each worker feel more accountable for his/her performance. Often direct supervisors/inspectors can be eliminated.

Quality of working life. Some plants have experienced improvements in workers' attitudes and performance as a result of the introduction of an AGV system. Likewise, absenteeism rates have decreased as have job-related injuries. This is all reflected in improved product quality.

Product quality. Because of less damage in handling and improved worker performance, product quality is often improved when using AGVs. This is reflected in less scrap, less repair, and in improved customer satisfaction.

These factors may not have the same benefits in all applications, and, in some, may not even be worthy of consideration. Each system has its own unique requirements and other variables that may alter the importance of these factors. At the same time, other factors not even listed may have considerable impact on the economics of such a system, either in a positive or negative sense. In order to provide an economic justification for the installation of a particular system, a complete analysis of the manufacturing system must be performed.

A logical approach to the justification process is to choose a base system for comparison purposes. A reasonable choice is probably the system used in the past, for example, a monorail system. Both qualitative and quantitative factors must be assessed for importance and taken into account. An AGV system will be difficult to justify economically on the grounds of labour savings alone – experience has shown only about 10–15% of the total system cost can be attributed to labour savings. As mentioned previously, it is difficult to put a monetary value on many of the factors listed. It is often possible at least to make an 'educated guess' by studying past history. For example, if employees have a high rate of sick leave because of back problems the vehicles may be designed to accommodate the workers and help eliminate this problem, thus producing monetary savings. Also, if a lot of inventory is lost or misplaced, the record keeping provided by the AGV system may be able to reduce material inventory substantially. By careful analysis of past expenses and of savings experienced by other AGV users, it is usually possible to establish some reasonable expected monetary savings.

Investment always involves risk, but through the use of good appraisal techniques the uncertainties can be reduced. All that can be done is to use appraisal techniques with common sense and discretion so that one proposed material-handling system is shown to be more likely to prove better or worse than another. All appraisal results rely on the accuracy of the input data, much of which is an estimation based on the experience of others. Probably one of the most comforting thoughts is that experience has shown that many existing users, after using AGVs for a while, decide to expand their systems to include other operations, because of the success of their original AGV system. For those considering using AGVs for the first time, it would be wise to make visits to existing users.

Example justification

An automobile manufacturer required a new final body assembly line. Two systems that could be successfully implemented and meet their production requirements were evaluated. The systems were required to accommodate both manual and automated (robots) assembly operations. The two systems compared were a sequential system (drag-chain conveyors with skuks and pedestals) and an asynchronous system (AGV system). The proposed AGV system utilised parallel path processing with stop-go stations for both manual and automated operations. The sequential system was specified to have stop-go stations for automated operations and a fixed sequential moving line for manual operations. Specific objectives for the system design were:

- Improve product quality.
- Ability to process for the product rather than the facility.
- Reduce jobs-in-system inventory.
- Minimise impact of production schedule fluctuations.
- Improve quality of working life.

To be able to evaluate each system on an equal basis, a series of tables containing the variables were developed. Each of these tables was used for a comparison and the corresponding savings determined. Four tables presented the costings and savings involved in using either a sequential system or an AGV system, under the categories of investment, manpower, floor-space, and operations.

In this case study, it turned out that the initial investments were almost equivalent, but the AGV system offered many advantages. However, a critic of this book took exception to this and stated "I don't care what or whose data you used, AGV systems cost two to three times more and require 30% more floor-space." Utilising parallel path processing achieves better line balance, less need for inspection and repair areas, and accommodates modular assembly more readily. There was also a reduction in direct labour, improved product quality, and improved worker environment.

In summary:

This chapter has presented several factors to be considered when evaluating an AGV system. Most systems are difficult to justify economically on initial investment or labour savings; however, AGV systems offer multitudes of other advantages that can be used for justification. Some of the factors produce tangible economic advantages whereas others are intangible in nature. Intangible factors make it difficult to determine a monetary savings value, and yet they will definitely affect the overall economic results. By referring to past data on the various factors and combining this information with expected improvements as experienced by other users, a good estimation can often be made. It is important to realise that not all AGV systems can be justified in the same manner, using the same factors. Every system is unique and a comparison study should be performed for each case.

Chapter Eight

System simulation

The success of any AGV system is highly dependent on the quality of the system design. Owing to the complexity of most AGV systems and to the number of variables within the material-handling system requirements, traditional engineering analysis methods are not sufficient for design and evaluation. With the advent of sophisticated computer-controlled material-handling systems, such as AGV systems, overhead electrified monorail and AS/RS, the need has arisen for more accurate and comprehensive engineering design techniques to be able to meet the system objectives. These objectives are:

- Prove the feasibility of the system design.
- Eliminate traffic problems.
- Increase system throughput given resource constraints.
- Reduce required inventory levels.
- Increase equipment utilisation through balancing.
- Maximise the system flexibility.
- Minimise the product cost.

Typically, randomness is inherent to AGV systems, and with randomness comes complexity. As the complexity of AGV systems increases, the potential for applying tried and true analytical techniques to make accurate assessments diminishes. Thus, 'simulating' or modelling the AGV system on a computer becomes an attractive alternative.

Computer simulation has become a powerful analytical tool that is able to help the engineer to design and verify the operation of complex handling systems. Several factors have contributed to growth in the popularity of simulation: firstly, dedicated simulation languages have been developed that are more user friendly; secondly, the 'computing power' has increased and, as a result, costs of building, running, and analysing models have decreased, so that computer simulation has become a more cost-justifiable design and analysis tool; and thirdly, animation of computer models has attracted many new supporters of simulation. The ability to see a proposed material-handling system on a screen provides the modeller with a tool to help verify the accuracy of his/her logic and to be able to 'sell' the results.

Computer simulation can provide reliable, comprehensive predictions to proposed or existing material-handling systems in a timely manner. This is accomplished at relatively low cost as compared to the cost of experimenting and changing existing systems until the desired state has been obtained. Successful simulation applications are abundant, and for many complex systems, simulation is no longer optional but rather a requirement.

Why use simulation?

A simulation of a system is necessary if the system exhibits a degree of randomness or complexity that precludes the use of analytical techniques. When applicable, analytical techniques are preferred to simulation because they provide exact answers. Such techniques include velocity and acceleration equations along with laws of physics and mechanics. Often, the random nature of a system is ignored which lessens or eliminates the requirement for simulation.

The results generated from simulation will give the engineer a clearer understanding of the behaviour of complex systems. Simulation also enables the user to compress time so that many hours of operation can be obtained in a few minutes. This allows for long-term system evaluation to determine where potential problems and system deficiencies may exist.

When to use simulation

Project phases when simulation can be used to improve the design and implementation of a material-handling system include:

- System design stages – configuration phase; analysis phase; operational phase.

- System implementation and control stages – training phase; emulation phase.

System design

Simulation is useful in the design process of all stages throughout the life of the material-handling system.

Configuration phase. This is the period of time between the initial concept of the system and the drawing of a firm layout. During this phase, many systems may be considered for the material handling. Analyses are usually rough, with many assumptions being made. Goals of simulation at this point include determining general flow characteristics of the system and estimating the number of vehicles required. Also, interactions between the material-handling system and other equipment in the facility are noted for future detailed consideration.

Analysis phase. The analysis phase runs on from the configuration phase and continues through to the start of production. All AGV system and control characteristics are modelled during this phase, including equipment reliability and processing data. Information obtained can include, but is not limited to, the following:

- Number of AGVs required to meet production goals.
- Buffer sizes.
- Allowable cycle times in workstations.
- Reliability and repair times of equipment in the system.
- Equipment utilisation.
- Verification that actual vehicle control logic will meet production goals.
- Verification of traffic flow.
- Assurance that the system is consistent with future production plans (for example, expansion with minimal additional investment).

This is usually considered the most important phase of the system design project since the information can be used for layout refinements. Because of this importance, the model is expected to predict accurately the performance of the system being analysed. However, it is important to recognise that the predictions made by the model reflect the accuracy of the data and the assumptions on which it was built. The art and science of simulation adhere strictly to the 'GIGO' principle, i.e., 'garbage in – garbage out'! For this reason it is important to obtain input design parameters and characteristics from those parties who are most familiar with the system. (Although the information provided by engineers, designers, and the AGV suppliers may not lead to accurate numerical conclusions, the model will still be of value. Even a poor simulation can provide insights into the performance and inter-dependencies of the proposed system.)

Operational phase. The final design considerations are assessed during the operational phase. This period begins at the start of production and continues throughout the life of the system. Simulations made at this time are generally conducted in-house and incorporate data obtained from the existing system. The model acts as a test-bed for examining the effects of equipment changes and new operational philosophies. The goal at this point is generally to improve the performance of the system.

System implementation and control

The benefits of simulation are not limited to the design aspects, as they are also of great value to the actual operation and control stage of an AGV system.

Training. Simulation can be an invaluable tool in training personnel in the operation of the AGV system. The impact of poor quality or maintenance in the system can be reflected in simulation output and shown to anyone participating in the operation. Animation and interactive capabilities of simulation programs will allow the user to make changes as the model is running and to see immediately the impact of those changes. Familiarity with the behaviour of the system can be gained by 'playing' with such a model.

Emulation. This refers to modelling an existing system in real-time. This is accomplished by monitoring system data and entering it into the model. The primary goals of emulation are: to monitor performance of the system in real-time; to model various control or operational philosophies, when undesirable conditions exist, to determine the most appropriate action; and to implement the most desirable action immediately. Although relatively new, emulation promises to be a valuable tool in day-to-day plant operations and in factories of the future.

System input design variables

AGV systems represent one of the more complex industrial devices to design and model.[7] The majority of time spent in any simulation process involves the gathering and definition of inputs. These can be divided into three categories, physical or spatial, time-related, and logical, all of which are important input requirements to consider and model in any AGV system simulation exercise.

Physical or spatial inputs are few and intuitively obvious: guidepath layout and control point layout.

Time-related inputs are often the most difficult of the inputs to assess. As a general rule, if a system characteristic takes time in real life, it should be considered for simulation purposes. If there is doubt as to the importance of a parameter, it should be included in the model. The parameter can be varied and its relative effect on the output can be determined. If it has significant effect, care should be taken to represent the parameter as accurately as possible. If the effect is minimal, it is not an important concern. Time-related inputs can include, but are not limited to, the following:

- Velocities (maximum, curve, creep, and loaded versus unloaded).
- Accelerations and decelerations.
- Communication requirements.
- Charging requirements.
- Positioning time.
- Work platform time (for example lift and lower times).
- Workstation characteristics (such as cycle times, time between failure, down-time, and set-up times).

Logical inputs, like the physical or spatial inputs, are relatively easy to determine. A system is usually designed with definite control strategies in mind and there is little ambiguity about them. Logical inputs generally include, but are not limited to, the following:[8]

- *Collision avoidance or blocking.* To ensure that no two vehicles try to occupy the same position at the same time, AGV systems must employ blocking protocols. A blocking scheme similar to the railway industry is employed. Control points are established along the guidepath, breaking the guidepath into segments. The central controller knows the location of all the vehicles in the system. Before a vehicle can enter a given segment, the segment must have no other vehicles present. The control points and blocking logic must be as close to the implementation design as possible to ensure model accuracy.

- *Courses and road maps.* These maps control the routing for each vehicle in the network. The routes outline how the vehicle will move through the facility. Decisions must also be made concerning route selection when more than one path exists between a vehicle and its destination. The simulation must reflect these routes as accurately as possible.

- *Dispatch and scheduling algorithms.* For optimum performance, it is critical that vehicles be routed for optimum response to upcoming load arrivals. This requires sophistication of dispatch and scheduling algorithms of the AGV network. The use of special dispatching rules can dramatically improve system performance and must be reflected in the simulation models.

- *En route protocol.* In the event that a portion of the AGV guidepath comes under contention, priority assignments are given to each vehicle. This interference may be between vehicles within the system or between an AGV and an external interference, such as a fork-truck. When there is a possibility of interference, the protocol will prevent both collision and a condition known as 'grid lock' – this arises when two vehicles have direct irresolvable interference from each other while attempting to perform their respective tasks.

- *Scheduling algorithms for the product.* As a vehicle transfers its load, the load status is also transferred. These vehicle actions must be modelled with appropriate timing.

- *Look-for-work.* On completion of a task the vehicle must look for work to acquire its next task. These algorithms increase in complexity with more flexible systems, since flexibility generally nullifies the tendancy to dedicate vehicles to specific routes.

- *Idle status protocol.* When there is no assignment for a given vehicle, it should be parked and placed in idle status. This can occur while the vehicle is waiting for station cycle completions, during breaks, and between shifts. There should be at least one parking place for each vehicle to prevent congestion in the network. The most effective parking places are adjacent to high activity areas.

● *Lane selection.* For assembly-type systems, many different rules are used in lane selection when vehicles are approaching parallel stations. Rules are typically based on such parameters as alternating selection, station status, queue contents, cumulative work performed, and job content.

Any one of the aforementioned inputs can be considered fixed or variable, depending on the circumstances and the latitude given to the system designers. One of the most important points to remember about modelling is that the accuracy of the results of a simulation model are directly related to the accuracy of the inputs and assumptions used in its development.

Information provided by simulation

Three major areas of information can be derived from simulation: time-related output, number-related output, and utilisation of resources. [2]

Time-related outputs may include, but are not limited to, the following:

● *Time to move.* This is the time which elapses while a job makes its way between any two points in the system and is a function of acceleration and deceleration times, maximum velocity, distance travelled, and curve times.

● *Time in a workstation.* This relates to the actual operation of the AGV at a station. The vehicle may have a raise and lower time when loading or unloading material, or it may be at an assembly station where the time is dictated by the actual assembly operation.

● *Delay time.* This is the time that elapses as a result of blockage or other delays, such as resequencing. When using asynchronous and synchronous lines together, some delays are encountered in resequencing the jobs from the asynchronous line (AGV) to the synchronous line.

Number-related outputs included such items as:

● *Number of jobs.* This consists of the number of jobs entering the system, the number of jobs in a queue or backed up waiting for a particular operation, and the number of jobs finished. A stable queue is one that will grow and recede within bounds. Ones that show continual accumulation produce an unstable condition and should be examined and corrected. Likewise, the jobs finished should be similar in number to the jobs input to the system.

- *Number of job types.* Jobs passing a particular point can be counted by job type and used as an indicator for jobs that require repair.

- *Number of vehicles.* The number of vehicles en route to a particular station are tallied as well as the number of vehicles being utilised by the system. With this information, the correct number of vehicles needed for a given throughput can be determined.

Utilisation of resources involves:

- *Utilisation of AGVs.* This will give an indication of the vehicles needed to support a given system and the required job rate. Either too many or too few vehicles can reduce the job throughput (too many causing traffic jams and too few allowing jobs to pile up), causing the system to become unstable.

- *Over/under utilisation.* This will show the percentage utilisation of any resources in the system and will point out areas or devices that will cause bottleneck situations.

Who should perform the simulation?

Depending on the complexity of the proposed system, the availability of in-house simulation capabilities, time limitations, and available finances, the simulation may be performed either by in-house personnel, consultants, or the AGV system vendor, and each has its own benefits and drawbacks.[9]

In-house personnel. The major advantage of this is that the simulation user will have an excellent understanding of the problem and be able to test vendor claims. Also, the facility will have the model and thus the capability to perform system implementation and control (training and emulation). The disadvantages are, with the exception of a few large companies, that the users will have to purchase simulation software or develop it themselves, making the initial cost high, and the initial development time considerable.

Consultants. There are many consulting firms that specialise in simulating material-handling systems such as AGV systems. These specialised consultants will have a good understanding of the problems and solutions, have experience in various industries, provide short development times, be able to test vendor claims, and do it at lower costs. The negative side is that the time required to test changes will be greater than it would be if using in-house capabilities, and even more important is that consultants do not have responsibility for implementation. This makes the detailed engineering of the analysis phase simulation more difficult.

AGV system vendors. Using vendors to provide simulations has many advantages. The vendor will have a good understanding of the problem and solutions, a close working relationship with the software group so that the detailed engineering stage can easily be accomplished, and responsibility for system implementation and the ability to do this at a lower cost. The major disadvantage is that the vendor may tend to sell solutions that support its own products.

The selection of in-house simulation over outside services by vendors or consultants would be feasible only if frequent simulations are required, there are personnel capable of providing the software, and if the necessary hardware (computing power) exists. Otherwise, if any of the following requirements or conditions exist, it would be better to make use of external services:

- No previous simulation experience.
- Infrequent simulation needs.
- No qualified personnel.
- Very complex material-handling system.
- Short development time required.

Simulation languages

The three phases of development (configuration, analysis and operation) require different levels of detail which also require different simulation languages. The best language for the situation needs to be evaluated. It is imperative, however, to remember that the modeller is still more important than the language used. For any given application, multiple languages are available and the appropriate language must be selected by the modeller.

```
VARIABLES IN THE MODEL
========================

NUMBER OF AGVS        40
DOWNTIME 1=YES         1
PERCENT WELD REPAIR  0.01


AGV CONTROL VARIABLES
----------------------------------------------------

RAISE TIME           0.0166  MINUTES
ACCELERATION TIME    0.0600  MINUTES
DECELERATION TIME    0.0600  MINUTES
CURVE TIME           0.0980  MINUTES
MAX SPEED          200.000   FT/MINUTE


NUMBER OF AGVS PER HOUR

ENTRIES IN TABLE    MEAN ARGUEMENT    STANDARD DEVIATION
       160              39.531               2.360


NUMBER OF AGVS PER DAY

ENTRIES IN TABLE    MEAN ARGUEMENT    STANDARD DEVIATION
        20             316.250               7.203


        ====================================

                    IN MINUTES
```

STN NAME	AVE STN CYCLE TIME	AVE WORK TIME	AVE BLOCKED TIME	INDEX TIME	PERCENT REPAIR TIME	NUMBER OF FAILURES
STN009	0.4943	0.0000	0.0157	0.4786	0.0000	0
STN010	0.6419	0.4500	0.0025	0.1770	0.8229	3
STN019	0.2499	0.0000	0.0090	0.2409	0.0000	0
STN020	0.6843	0.5000	0.0016	0.1791	0.2396	11
STN021	0.7056	0.4999	0.0001	0.2056	0.0000	0
STN025	0.4517	0.0000	0.0002	0.4515	0.0000	0
STN029A	0.3513	0.0000	0.0001	0.3512	0.0000	0
STN030A	1.4063	1.2297	0.0000	0.1766	0.0000	0
STN031A	0.4775	0.0000	0.0376	0.4399	0.0000	0

Fig. 8.1   Typical tabular display of simulation results

Languages should provide the following features: model development speed, model accuracy, model communication, model usefulness, and modeller training. It is desirable that the simulation language provide for on-line changes so that system modifications can quickly be entered to see their effect on the system. It is also important to consider the format in which the results will be displayed – some tabular forms (Fig. 8.1) are difficult to interpret whereas graphical displays (Fig. 8.2) quickly show problem areas.

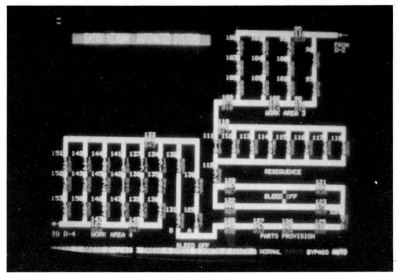

Fig. 8.2 Graphical display of simulation results

Table 8.1 Comparison of simulation language types

Category	Examples	Advantages	Disadvantages
Scientific	Fortran PL/1 Pascal Basic	Flexible Adaptable Familiar to programmers	Costly labour hours High programmer skills Not user friendly Output not easily understood

General
purpose
	GPSS
	SLAM II
	SIMSCRIPT
		Application flexibility
		Engineering orientated
			Programmer skills
			Hardware requirements
			Trade-off between time
			  required and model
			  detail

Special
purpose
	Speed
	MAP/1
	Gentle
	Most
	Habms
	K&T FMS
	  simulator
	VMS
		Low programming skill
		Short programming time
		Often runs on
		  microcomputer
		Operated by common
		  user
			Lack of flexibility
			Will not simulate entire
			  system

MACRO	Simon Automod KMG	Model development speed Model accuracy Low programming skill English language syntax Model communication	Lack of flexibility 'Black box' fear

The importance of the language is dependent upon the modeller's simulation skill, his/her industrial skill, the detail required, and the relative importance of the decision making based on the model outcome. Simulation languages available can be categorised into four types: scientific, general purpose, special purpose, and MACRO. Table 8.1 gives examples of each language along with it associated advantages and disadvantages. [10]

Once again, it is emphasised that the modeller is more important than the language used. Successful application of simulation requires skills from a number of disciplines, including computer science, mathematics, and statistics, and an understanding of the industrial systems involved. It is a combination of both art and science. Knowing how to use the latest simulation language does not guarantee that models will be built correctly and provide accurate answers that aid decisions.

Future trends

The future of AGV system simulation holds much promise. Special-purpose simulation languages will continue the trend toward easier use while simultaneously the cost will continue to decrease. Graphics will play an increasing role with improved colourgraphics input and display systems integrated directly into simulation languages and simulation output processors. Much of this is directly related to the continued increase in capability of microcomputers. Integrated databases will link to the factory database input for more comprehensive output analysis. Software integration will link simulation with other management software tools allowing for real-time on-line simulation and real-time decision making.

In summary:

Simulation is an integral part of factory automation. Simulation animation satisfies an essential need to validate and communicate system concepts. Except for the simplest possible systems, simulation should be considered a necessity and not an option. One simulation consultancy claims that every simulation it has performed has resulted in considerable cost savings for the user.

The first step in performing an AGV system simulation is identifying the analysis objectives. Typical objectives are to maximise throughput while minimising the number of AGVs. Other objectives may include the input of manual fork-truck interference on the system. Obviously, the more specific the objectives, the more detailed the model that is required.

The development of new AGV systems requires three phases: configuration, analysis and operation. The configuration phase is mainly for comparison of the options for the basic system. Simulation is performed quickly, kept simple, and is usually done by the system designer. In the analysis phase, the physical plant layout is generated. The guidepaths, location of the work modules, and material-handling system are established. Simulation requires more detail to determine if the system will perform. The operation phase is referred to as the 'flight simulator'. All details, including scheduling, are established and simulation is in the 'what-if?' stage. The use of on-line graphics and animation makes it possible to visualise the consequences of the what-if? analysis. Simulation requires the utmost detail with regard to scheduling.

Once the final model is generated, the variables of the system can be manipulated to find optimum performance. Common variables are the number of AGVs in the system and whether down-time will be introduced. Down-time is a difficult variable in simulation because it is only derived from estimates.

Chapter Nine

System specification

Writing the specification for an AGV system can be an involved and complex process, and should not be taken lightly. AGV systems are much more complex than other material-handling devices. Selection of the type of controller, its capabilities, interfacing requirements, and back-up, are all important user decisions. The vehicle requirements, in terms of work-platform design, function, safety devices, and cycle time, all have to be specified. These, and a multitude of other variables not experienced when using other forms of material-handling devices, must be well defined in order for a supplier to give a firm quote. The user needs to have a good understanding of what the facility's material-handling requirements are and what is expected from the AGV system. Such items as electrical control, monitoring and report generation, control system, computer and computer-system interfacing, vehicle, acceptance procedure, training, and general plant specifications, all need to be specified.

Owing to the complexity and newness of AGV system applications a first-time user must select, in advance of order placement, a supplier with which to work closely. A supplier will assist in developing:

- The AGV system functional specification.
- A workable guidepath layout which takes into account through-puts, traffic patterns, vehicle sweeps, interfaces with other machines, immovable objects, and payload considerations.
- The vehicle functional specification.
- Control system requirements (as detailed in Chapter Five).

It must be understood that individual AGV designs can affect each of these points. Therefore, selection of a potential supplier to act as an engineering consultant is critical. This supplier/ consultant can also provide budgetary pricing information.

This chapter presents many of the factors that need to be determined under each of the listed specification items. This is intended to be a guide to the items that should be covered in a complete specification to achieve satisfactory results.

Vehicle specifications

This section outlines the important specification items relating to the vehicle design and operation. It should be noted that they are all suggested items, and are by no means all-inclusive. The items to be specified will vary from system to system depending on the application requirements, types of vehicles needed, and the type of guidepath desired.

Vehicle control. The expected on-board computed functions of the vehicle should be determined. For example, are the vehicles to be capable of performing to some extent without the main controller? Are the vehicles required to know where they are? Are they to be able to restart from the floor level after power or system failure? Are the vehicles to contain self-diagnostics? Are they to be able to receive operating commands from the sub-host and interpret and execute them? Are they to be able to perform timing functions?

Vehicle construction. The environment that the vehicles are to operate in should be specified along with any special vehicle requirements. For example, is the vehicle to operate in a wet environment and is it to be sealed to prevent dust, water, or oil from causing failures? Does the vehicle need to have access panel doors, quick disconnects, plug-in modular controls, battery trays equipped with rollers? Should it provide lift lugs for maintenance? Should the sharp edges exposed to operators or maintenance personnel be removed or rounded?

Drive requirements. Requirements such as wheel material and suspension are specified. For example, the wheel material might be polyurethane with a composite to provide traction on wet floors; the wheel suspension is to keep all wheels in contact, assuming the floor is level within a ¾in. tolerance.

External appearance. Here such items as vehicle colour, warning labels, and identification numbers are specified.

Vehicle operation. Specifications need to be provided for all operational requirements, such as: manual override of all functions by use of the pendant; motions required in the manual mode (i.e. forward/backward) and the automatic mode; speed range; gradients to be encountered; easy removal from the system by hand pushing and steering; metal expansion joint distance that the vehicle is expected to cross; and incorporation of 'sleep' mode to facilitate extensive periods of down-time with sufficient battery life for proper start up.

Batteries and charging. This is such a complex issue, dependent upon so many variables, that the user will probably need to rely upon the supplier for guidance. AGV duty cycles, along with vehicle design and construction, are fundamental components of the type of charging scheme used and the batteries to be specified. (The various battery-charging techniques are discussed in greater detail in Chapter Three.)

Specification items include type of batteries (e.g. maintenance-free), vehicle cycle requirement (e.g. operate 17-hour shift/day), type of charging (e.g. opportunity charge in station or full-cycle), special charging receptacle requirements (e.g. recessed and protected from plant environment), charging verification desired (e.g. automatic or with human intervention).

Safety. The following safety requirements might be specified:

- Emergency stop/start buttons readily accessible on both sides of vehicle.
- Emergency bumpers and ride bumper extensions must be able to stop the vehicle before the bumper fully compresses.
- Turn signals and brake lights to warn pedestrians of vehicle movements.
- Protection from running over operator's foot.
- Guarding of all pinch points.
- Control provision to maintain proper spacing between vehicles.
- Provisions to stop vehicle before any part (including load), comes in contact with any obstacles or another vehicle.
- Fail-safe capability to stop vehicle in event of mechanical or electrical failure (loss of signal and any condition that could result in hazardous situations).

- Vehicle must be able to maintain load in any position in the event of power failure.

Work platform. If the vehicle does not have standard off-the-shelf work platform, complete details need to be given as to functions and expected operation of the work platform. For example, if a vehicle is expected to carry a chassis and lift it into the body of a car, the complete chassis layout, its weight, and required lift height must all be specified.

Prototype vehicle. If the vehicle required is not standard, the supplier should provide one or two prototype vehicles that are representative of production models. They should be put through all system performances at the supplier's facility, and any non-conformance should be rectified prior to final build release.

Facility control function specifications

This section deals with specifications for the facility control functions that will be required of the system. It will probably be necessary to specify the type of computer desired and the configuration required so that it can be integrated into the existing network. Also, the level of back-up and data storage needs to be defined.

System host controller

The functions of the host level need to be determined and specified. Some of the possible functions include:

- *Load tracking/job description* – This is the concept of locating and identifying any load in the system. This method of describing the load identification and characteristics, as well as the method of data input need to be defined.
- *Flexible scheduling/broadcast requirements* – How will necessary information be transmitted to the workstations and material kitting areas? How will the necessary parts be identified?
- *Reporting* – Exact report types, format, and generation capabilities need to be specified.
- *Editing and updating* – The purpose of this is to allow the user to change application programs and system status data. Questions such as who will be permitted to do this and how the changes are to be entered need to be addressed.

- *Routing order* – Generation of a routing order occurs when a request is made to move a load within a facility. The sources of these requests (including manual ones) need to be specified. Also, the information that the orders should provide should be determined.
- *Routing sequence definition* – The structure of the routing sequence, such as matching load identities against specific workcell capabilities, needs to be defined, along with routing order generation and integrity check methods.
- *Workcell definition* – This will describe the configuration of all workcells in a system and includes such items as station identification, cycle times associated with that station, acceptable job types, and cell description.
- *Security and access control* – It needs to be determined who has access to the system and at what levels. For example, level 1 may have report and query capabilities only, whilst at the top level access to any part of the system may be permissible, including changing programs, account numbers, and passwords.
- *External system interfaces* – All the other systems, networks, and automation with which the AGV system will be required to interface should be listed.
- *System diagnostics* – The extent of diagnostics expected and the type of display desired should be defined
- *Facility layout parameters* – This includes the generation and maintenance of communication-point locations, stop-point locations, station locations, intersection information, interference-point locations, and possible frequencies to be followed.
- *Hold/resume functions* – Requirements need to be defined relating to the ability to hold a vehicle, generate new orders, and resume its operation.
- *Sleep mode* – It is necessary to specify how the system is to put vehicles in a sleep mode and wake them up when they are needed. It is also necessary to specify sleep locations.
- *User interface* – The type of interface desired, types of transactions, and access methods should be described.

Floor controllers

The desired functions of the floor controller need to be specified. These may include:

- *Service of transport orders* – Including the receipt and queueing of orders on a priority scheme, if necessary.

- *System traffic management* – Including carrier selection, system blocking, and lane selection.
- *Error reporting* – Used to log all error conditions encountered for system management reporting.
- *Vehicle command formatting* – Appropriate vehicle commands from the routing orders need to be formatted. This should include such commands as order number, exact destination, timing requirements, and special instructions for any given workstation.
- *System status display* – The type of display (e.g. graphical) and contents of the display should be specified.
- *Transport order completion communication* – For example, following the completion of every transport order, the facility's host controller is notified so that it can be stored in the memory.
- *Communication with vehicles* – The expected commands and data to be communicated as well as the baud rate should be defined.
- *Communication with facility's host controller* – The minimum baud rate and list of information to be communicated should be specified.
- *Control of vehicle charging* – The control must be responsible for initiating the type and method of charging selected.

Vehicle control functions

The vehicles (if intelligent-type) should be specified to perform the following functions:

- *Queue commands* – The carrier needs to be capable of accepting multiple commands from the control system. The number and type of commands need to be specified.
- *Interpret and execute commands* – The vehicle needs to be able to interpret and execute commands selected sequentially from a queue.
- *Communication of status* – The vehicle needs to communicate its status information to the control system. Possible information to be specified may include carrier number, battery level, task being executed, last communication point identity, next communication point identity, safety faults encountered, and current location.

- *Manual control pendant* – Vehicles should be able to perform all functions manually via the control pendant and without need of the vehicle microprocessor.
- *Receive 'map' down-load* – A vehicle should be capable of accepting the facility layout map to allow it to know where it is at all times and to run in a degraded mode if the system controllers fail.
- *Work-cycle timing* – The vehicle will know the appropriate time required for its load and workstation and initiate automatic release.
- *Operate without system controllers* – The vehicles should be capable of operating without the system controllers. The vehicle should maintain the status records so when the control system is reactivated, the records will be able to be transferred and not lost.

Software development and documentation

Software

The number of copies of the required software should be specified along with the method, e.g. tape, disks, or other storage methods. Other considerations include:

- Narrative description and computer-generated listings with line-by-line comments.
- Documentation to include a flow-chart showing hierarchy and execution sequence.
- Index for all programs required.
- Description of step-by-step procedure for modifying program.
- Determination of the language in which all application programs are to be written.

Manuals

The number of copies and the form (e.g. hard copy) need to be specified. Types of manuals should include:

- Operators' manuals which cover such procedures as how to start the system, how to use each function, and description of databases and how to maintain them.
- Implementation manuals which enable the system engineers to install and maintain the software, and provide step-by-step

instructions on how to build the runnable system from source modules and module description sheets.

- Maintenance manuals which contain sufficient detail to allow maintenance of all components, e.g. troubleshooting and modifying software and troubleshooting and replacing hardware.

Other specifications

Other specifications that need to be determined and listed include training commitments by the supplier, acceptance procedure, and general plant specifications (e.g. structural steel, pneumatic equipment, painting, and piping). These specifications are not necessarily unique to AGV systems, so the standard specifications used by an existing facility will probably be sufficient.

In summary:

The specification overview presented in this chapter followed the pattern of that used to specify an AGV system used in an assembly operation. Obviously a specification for an AGV material-handling system using tuggers or pallet trucks will be somewhat different. However, the general topic areas will be the same, and many of the items are still valid. The intention of this chapter was not to develop a specification but rather give a general idea of items that should be considered.

Chapter Ten

System implementation

The implementation of AGV systems, as with all other high-tech devices, requires special considerations. Many of these devices do not conform to the image of 'standard machinery', and thus create apprehension among personnel, from line workers through to managers. The 'fear of the unknown' syndrome tends to prevail. There is often fear even among the engineers in charge of such an undertaking because the system selected is the first of a kind. There is always the question as to whether one should 'play safe' with old and well-tried methods, or venture out with the new. Even if one is positive that AGVs offer the best solution to a facility's material-handling problems, it is often difficult to proceed with confidence. This chapter outlines a procedure that could help to minimise problems associated with implementing a system.

Implementation considerations

Personnel. It is imperative that all personnel who will be directly or indirectly involved with the AGV system be familiarised as to what the system is and how it will affect them. In the past, AGV systems have been forced out of facilities because of worker sabotage. As discussed previously in Chapter Two, management support is just as important as worker support – without commitment from all levels of management, from the line supervisor to top management, the system could be doomed to failure. Training seminars should be designed for each level of management as well as for the line workers; these seminars should provide such information as why an AGV system is being considered, its advantages over conventional material-handling systems, potential problem areas, and what is expected in terms of support from that particular group being trained. If the expertise to provide such a training seminar does not exist within a facility, an AGV supplier or independent consultancy should be approached.

Application. When considering implementing an AGV system, it is important to select the most suitable first application. Failure to do so can cause insurmountable problems. Failure of the system to operate will cause frustration at all personnel levels, along with a 'bad feeling' toward AGV systems. One bad experience with a new technology can result in the writing-off of that technology as 'no good', thus potentially making the plant obsolete.

Often, engineers or managers will visit a facility similar to their own and see the entire material-handling system automated, using a very complex AGV system. Likewise, they may attend a material-handling seminar or see a film on such a system. It should be realised that these systems were put together in stages over many years and that a team of engineers would have been assigned who spent months or even years visiting applications around the world and studying all aspects of the system before proceeding. It is important to start out with a manageable system and one that can be understood by the facility's personnel. Future system requirements should also be considered with a view towards subunit integration and obsoletion. Also, the ability to expand may reflect system complexity – an application where the benefits are clearly visible will help convince management and workers of the real benefits derived from using AGVs and that the system should be expanded.

Preliminary engineering. At this stage, as much information as possible is gathered about AGV systems used in similar applications. This will involve visits to AGV suppliers for information about their units and capabilities, and it should involve visits to other facilities that are using AGV systems in similar applications. The engineers should also learn of potential problem areas experienced by others. During this time, a study of all the facility's material-handling requirements should be accomplished, and a decision on how to integrate the AGV system should be made.

If the proposed system requires more than two vehicles, a basic simulation should be considered. This will give a rough idea of the system required, including the number of vehicles needed to meet the material-handling requirements. At this stage, the simulation can be relatively crude and is not intended to be a refined detail of the system.

Supplier selection. In order to implement an AGV system successfully, experience in North America and Europe indicates that a strong working relationship should exist between the supplier and user. Such a relationship needs to be developed before the order is placed. Supplier selection is crucial and must be done with great care. It is important to select suppliers that are likely to be in business for some time so that parts and service will be available – the supplier's reputation and financial backing are possible indicators. It is also important to obtain a list of installations that the supplier has designed and installed, and visits to those relevant made accordingly. Information should be sought as to the support and cooperation that the supplier provided during both the design and installation stages, and whether the supplier had the level of expertise necessary to design, help specify, build, and install the system.

Copies of the supplier's maintenance and operation manuals should be obtained and checked for their clarity and completeness. Yet another factor is evaluation of the supplier's training. Operational and maintenance personnel at a facility will need good training to be able to maintain the equipment and modify the system to meet changing and future needs. It is not recommended to rely upon the supplier for maintenance and system modifications; however, the supplier should offer such service if required. Another consideration is the responsiveness of the supplier in providing parts and service when requested.

Obviously, cost is an important factor but should not be the only consideration when selecting a supplier. Many of the other factors are subjective and are determined after interviewing other users and evaluating their reactions to the suppliers they have dealt with. Companies which deal only with sales should be avoided.

Preliminary justification. Based on the preliminary engineering and simulation, there should be enough information to obtain estimates from the various suppliers. Using this information along with tangible savings, it is possible to calculate both payback period and return on investment. If these results, together with other associated benefits (such as intangible savings, safety, ergonomics, and increased product quality) are sufficient to convince management, the project should then proceed to the next stage. (Chapter Two discusses possible justification factors.)

Detailed engineering. At this point, engineering involves determining exact system requirements, including all peripheral equipment such as transfer mechanisms, material stands, conveying units, interfacing devices, and other equipment necessary to make the system operate. Detailed specifications are needed for the carrier, including the on-board computing ability, load capacity, work-platform design, and the duty cycle between charging. The control requirement needs to be established as to how commands are entered – either manually or by the host computer. How to interface equipment, such as robots, AS/RS, and CNC machines, also needs to be determined, along with requirements for management reports, such as system status and material records. (The specifications for an AGV system are discussed in greater detail in Chapter Nine.) A complete project schedule, with complete details as to the plant's and supplier's responsibilities and deadlines, needs to be established.

System back-ups (control and vehicle) and manual back-up should both be considered. If manual back-up is provided, it should not be too convenient otherwise there may be little, if any, incentive to return the AGV system to service. Complete and detailed simulation should be accomplished, verifying that all the material-handling requirements will be met and that the number of vehicles will be sufficient to allow for vehicle down-time and charging time.

Finalised justification. With the detailed system specification completed, it is now possible to obtain finalised quotes for the AGV system and all peripheral equipment needed. Again, the payback and return on investment should be recalculated to ensure that it is still a viable project.

Ordering. When the final supplier is selected and the order is placed, it is wise to have penalty clauses in the contract. Penalties should be imposed for late delivery, especially if detrimental. Severe penalties or non-payment should be imposed if the system does not operate to specification. If the system is a turnkey operation, it is important that the engineers from the facility who are working with the supplier's engineers be involved in the design, build, and check-out phases. If this is not done, no one at the facility will understand the system and how it works after completion. After payment, suppliers tend to lose some of their enthusiasm in helping to troubleshoot the system.

Training. Training of operation and maintenance personnel should not be accomplished too far in advance of the system's arrival otherwise the training's effectiveness will be diminished – two or three weeks in advance of the system's arrival is ideal. If there is a longer timespan, much of the material covered will be forgotten. Also, personnel will be excited about applying what they have learned, and their enthusiasm will soon dwindle as time elapses. More training may also be required after the system is installed and debugged.

Site preparation. Correct preparation for the arrival of the AGV system can ensure a smooth transition from the present handling method to the new system. Coordination of every aspect that is required to merge the AGV system into the material-handling facility should be planned to cause the least disruption. Necessary rearrangement of conveyors, machines, and other devices should be made. Aisles and other necessary floor-space should be made ready, and the maintenance and charging areas should be built. Floor preparation may be necessary to provide a smooth, level concrete surface. Modifications required to existing equipment should be made, as long as it does not interfere with present production.

Installation. No matter how well any system is thought out and designed, problems will occur. There should be sufficiently trained in-house personnel as well as the supplier's expert personnel available during start-up so that any problems experienced may be corrected. Upper and middle management needs to be supportive and provide the manpower and other resources required to accomplish this. The project manager should have a firm understanding of what is required, a project schedule, and a firm commitment to see the project through to completion. With complex systems there will inevitably be more problems, and thus more support will be required. It is during this period that almost everyone involved with the project panics and wonders if it will ever come together – if sufficient managerial support exists, it will!

Debugging. Even after the system is operational, quirks will appear. These may range from small irritations to those that bring the entire system to a standstill. Some complex systems will have one or two resident experts from the supplier working with the system for several months to deal with such problems. Otherwise it is the project engineer's responsibility to troubleshoot.

Acceptance. An acceptance test procedure should be developed by both the user and supplier. Performance criteria need to be established, including the length of the test period. System purchase will follow a 'successful' acceptance test. If the test requirements are not sufficiently specified, acceptance may be forced on the user even with a partially operational system.

Evaluation. After the system has been debugged and operational for a few months, an evaluation of the system can be of considerable value in helping to design future systems. Unexpected benefits may appear which will help justify other systems. Likewise, problem areas become apparent, and when analysed possible solutions may become evident and improvements designed into future systems.

In summary:

For successful implementation of an AGV system, a carefully prepared procedure should be followed. One suggested procedure is to:

- Familiarise personnel with the new system proposal.
- Select the most suitable first application.
- Carry out a preliminary engineering exercise to gather information on other AGV systems.
- Select the most suitable supplier.
- Carry out a preliminary justification.
- Perform the detailed engineering for exact system requirements.
- Obtain firm quotes.
- Order the system.
- Train the operation and maintenance personnel.

- Prepare the site.
- Install the system.
- Debug the system.
- Carry out a system acceptance test.
- Evaluate the results with a view towards future system design.

Chapter Eleven

Overhead AGV systems

Another form of an AGV system being given much attention is the 'overhead powered monorail' or 'overhead AGVS' (also known as automated monorail, electrified monorail, computerised monorail, and self-propelled monorail carriers.[11]) As the names suggest, the powered monorail is a self-propelled vehicle which travels on a single overhead rail. Such overhead AGV systems have several inherent advantages and disadvantages compared with floor-travelling systems. This chapter describes the components of overhead AGV systems and their applications, and outlines these advantages and disadvantages.

System components

The major components of a powered monorail system are the trolley, the track, the switching devices and the electronic control system.

Trolley

The trolley, which actually transfers the material, consists of a motor, drive and idler trolleys, an on-board control unit, and a load bar to which the material-handling fixture is attached. Power for the motor is received via a bus-bar built into or above the track. The motors are generally of fractional horsepower and operate on three-phase power, typically between 24 and 48V. Since direction of travel is mechanically controlled by the track, the on-board electronics can be extremely simple. They are usually limited to forward/reverse directional control and vehicle speed control.

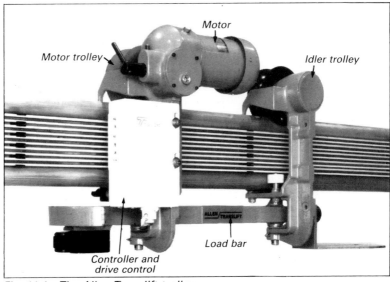

Fig. 11.1   The Allen Translift trolley

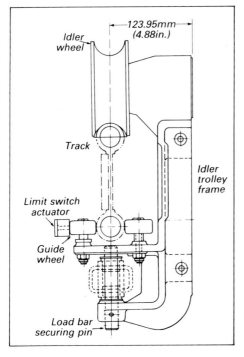

Fig. 11.2   Cross-section of the Allen Translift rail and trolley

This information is conveyed to the trolley from the central controller through the bus-bar.

The trolleys are capable of travelling at very high speeds (600ft/min, approx. 180m/min) with excellent positioning accuracy ($\pm$1cm). The positioning accuracy necessary for most robotic applications can then be accomplished with external fixturing.

The trolleys are also capable of handling very heavy loads. Typical capacities range from 100 to 5000lb (approx. 45–2250kg), although systems are available to handle loads up to 200,000lb (approx. 90,000kg). The only limiting factors are the power of the motor and the strength of the overhead steel support.

Fig. 11.1 shows an Allen Translift with a 1100lb (approx. 500kg) capacity. It is a two-speed unit, capable of travelling at 400ft/min (approx. 120m/min) between stations. The motor operates on 42V, three-phase power with the horsepower being determined by design requirements. Fig. 11.2 is a cross-section of the idler trolley and its relationship to the track.

Track

Track designs differ greatly depending on the manufacturer and the load-handling capacity. Generally, for low-capacity systems, extruded aluminium is used because of its light weight and ease of manufacturing. For higher-capacity systems, steel I-beams and C-channel are used. Tracking comes in standard lengths and girth which can be cut to any length required. Most manufacturers offer custom-built sections, but cost usually limits their use except where absolutely necessary.

Switching

The switching device is the method of routing control in an overhead AGV system. Fig. 11.3 shows the standard switching components utilised by most manufacturers. Specialised switching devices can be custom manufactured, but at significant extra cost. The first three devices in Fig. 11.3 (the Y-switch, the V-switch, and the three-way switch) allow multiple tracks to merge or a single track to diverge into multiple tracks. Common uses are parallel processing, a 'passing lane' to allow for bidirectional use of a single line, and a resequencing area. The fourth device, a cross-point, is used to allow two tracks to cross without a level change. The fifth device, a turntable, can send a trolley down one of several tracks. The sixth device, a side transfer switch, transfers

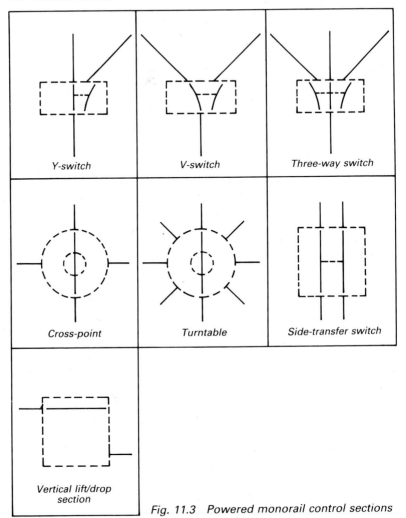

Fig. 11.3   Powered monorail control sections

a trolley to a parallel line. It is most commonly used for an off-line maintenance test loop. The last device, a vertical lift/drop section, allows for a large level change between tracks.

Control system

This is the most application-dependent component of a powered monorail system. A small programmable logic controller can operate a limited system with little switching and few trolleys, whereas more complex systems require a more complex controller; very large and complex systems often have a network of controllers tied into a central host computer.

Since overhead AGVs ride on a track, it allows the on-board trolley control unit to be comparatively simple. In most systems, its only functions are speed control, forward/reverse control and miscellaneous carrier control. In a floor AGV system, the controller must compensate for any wavering from the desired path which greatly increases the cost and complexity of the unit. However, in an overhead AGV system, the trolley merely goes where the track leads it. An excellent illustration is the difference between a car and a train. A car requires constant driver input to remain on course. The decision to turn left, right or continue straight, is made entirely by the driver within the confines of the available roadway. The train, of course, is very different inasmuch as its path is entirely controlled by the track.

Most applications require the tracking of trolleys throughout the production process, and this therefore increases the memory requirements of a control system. A bar-code mounted on the trolley can be read at critical points by a bar-code reader. The controller can then output to a switching device to determine the path any particular trolley should follow. Using this information, in addition to production records, can allow the resequencing of trolleys to synchronous lines.

The controller also tells the trolley to slow down, stop, or back up as it reaches a station. A series of limit switches can inform the controller of a trolley's location. When a particular switch is 'tripped' by the trolley on its approach to a station, the controller can communicate with the trolley via the bus-bar and make it slow down or stop. Another limit switch can be used to inform the controller that the trolley has overshot the station and make the trolley back up. When the task has been completed, the trolley can be released from the station manually, or if a robot is involved, released by the robot's controller.

Advantages and disadvantages

An overhead AGV system has several inherent advantages and disadvantages. Firstly, an overhead AGV system may be more expensive than standard conveyors – a moderately complex system can often exceed $1 million. However, many of its advantages may justify the high cost of the initial installation. One particular advantage over standard conveyors is the large degree of processing flexibility supporting asynchronous production.

A floor AGV system also allows this degree of flexibility, but there are other factors which may influence the decision in favour of an overhead AGV system. A major advantage is lower vehicle cost – an average floor AGV costs between $75,000 and $100,000, whereas an average overhead AGV trolley costs beween $3000 and $10,000. The large difference in price is because a monorail trolley has its path determined by the track, and the on-board control system is drastically simpler than that of a floor AGV. Also, a floor AGV also requires batteries which add to the vehicle cost.

However, the cost savings experienced in favour of the trolley vehicle are somewhat offset by the higher cost of monorail track.

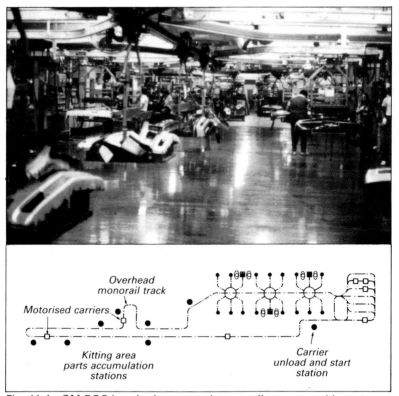

Fig. 11.4   *GM BOC Lansing's powered monorail system and layout*

A single switch costs more than the trolley unit itself, and a turntable or vertical lift may cost five to ten times the trolley cost. A floor AGV system requires only a smooth concrete floor with an embedded wire or painted strip for guidance. As a result, future layout changes are easier with a floor AGV system.

Nevertheless, with overhead AGV systems, floor-space is left uncluttered and there is less interference with other activities in the area – an obvious advantage. The trolley need only be at operator level when an operation is being performed on the item it is carrying. The overhead system also eliminates the need for the new, smooth floor required by a floor AGV system.

Overhead AGVs are also more suitable for very long runs. They are capable of considerably higher speeds than a floor AGV, which therefore reduces transfer time, the number of vehicles required, and work-in-progress inventory. Furthermore, there is no need for recharging with overhead AGVs because they are not dependent on batteries for power.

Another positive feature of overhead AGVs is their smooth, quiet operation. In all but the very large capacity models, the trolley travels on nylon wheels. This contributes to very low levels of noise in the work-place. In addition, the controlled trolley acceleration and the inherent smoothness of the track combine to give a very gentle ride for delicate items. Power conveyors and free conveyors are subject to starting and stopping shocks, and the slightest imperfection in the floor surface will jolt a floor AGV

Installation examples

There are numerous installations of overhead AGV systems in manufacturing plants. Two installations with greatly differing processing requirements are discussed below.

The first installation is a bumper assembly line at the GM BOC Lansing Plant in Lansing, Michigan (Fig. 11.4). The system has 1146ft (approx. 350m) of track and 46 trolleys. The process starts with the loading of a front and rear bumper onto the trolley. The trolley is then loaded with the parts necessary for the complete assembly of the bumper pair. From the loading station, the trolley then travels to one of the 18 assembly legs where a team of two assemblers completely assembles the bumper pair. Access to the 18 assembly legs is accomplished through the use of a trio of turntables. When the assembly is complete, the trolley is released by the operators and travels to the resequencing area. There,

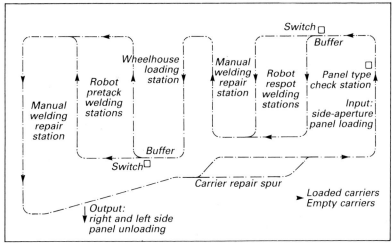

Fig. 11.5   The Chrysler powered monorail welding operation layout. The routing of monorail carriers through the system is controlled by a central programmable controller, while carrier moves are tracked by a control memory. Switches direct carriers to welding stations

through the use of bar-codes, the controller releases the completed bumpers to the main line in production sequence.

The assembly legs allow the flexibility to vary product mix. The system also helps to improve worker interest and quality since the worker is given several tasks to complete the entire bumper, and the repetitive nature of assembly-line work is reduced.

The second installation is the side-panel weld line at Chrysler's Fenton, Missouri plant. Fig. 11.5 shows the general layout of the welding operation. Overhead AGVs provide fast transfer between welding operations. A buffer is maintained ahead of the parallel welding stations, and when the welding cycle is complete the track is switched to the appropriate station and the trolleys simultaneously advance. This layout helps keep the welding robots busy for the maximum amount of time.

Electric track vehicles

The electric track vehicle (ETV) systems described in this section are basically a light-duty version of electrified monorails. They are primarily designed for use in electronics manufacturing, hospitals, and commercial buildings. ETV capabilities range from a maximum of 20–60lb (approx. 9–27kg) carrying capacity. They are

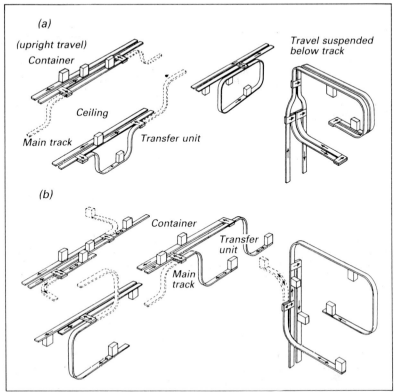

Fig. 11.6 ETV track configurations: (a) through station, and (b) reversing station

available in configurations from a simple point-to-point system through to multistation computer-controlled versions. The discussion of ETVs in this section is limited to the multistation computer-controlled version since these may be considered to be overhead AGVs.

The track on which the vehicles ride is approximately 8in. (approx. 20cm) wide, and is available in standard 10ft lengths (approx. 4.5m). Horizontal curves and vertical bends are also available to alter the direction of movement of the vehicle by the required angle. Unlike electrified monorails, ETVs have the capability of travelling up/down slopes as well as horizontally. However, the steeper the incline, the lesser the load capacity. At 90° (straight up), the ETV may only be able to carry about one-third of its normal rated load. If the full-rated load capacity is

Fig. 11.7   ETV system vehicles: (a) vehicle with fixed basket, (b) with self-levelling basket, and (c) with a large basket

needed for a vertical move, either the slope must be kept to a minimum (30–45°) or a vertical transport (elevator) needs to be used. Fig. 11.6 illustrates the various track configurations available.

The vehicles are powered with 24V dc obtained from the power rails mounted in the track section. They are driven horizontally with a friction wheel and vertically by a gear in the vehicle and a rack inserted in the track. Vehicles have bidirectional capabilities. Most ETVs are 8in. (approx. 20cm) wide and about 12–20in. (approx.30–50cm) in length (Fig. 11.7). Containers are mounted on the vehicles and are desgined to carry the product. They can be self-levelling which keeps the product in a horizontal position even during vertical movements. The containers can be wider and longer than the ETVs but allowance for this needs to be considered when the system layout is determined.

The controls consist of microprocessors for the vehicles, switches, and central controller. TransLogic's distributed processor controller can handle up to 254 service points (workstations, storage areas, etc.) and up to 254 vehicles. When dispatching a vehicle, the operator informs the central controller of the vehicle's identification number and its given destination point. This information is transferred to the switch microprocessors. When a switch identifies an approaching vehicle it will automatically switch to the proper position. This ensures that the ETV arrives at its given destination by the shortest possible route, and means that if a vehicle was to be removed from the system before reaching its destination, and then reinserted anywhere, the vehicle would still find its destination using the shortest possible route from its new starting point.

The central controller (CPU) continually communicates with the single-board computer controller located at each switching device in the system, using a polling technique. Instructions for car routing, dispatch and scheduling are downloaded, and status data including vehicle location, station and switch status are uploaded during the polling. The station displays are continuously updated on the CRT and traffic data is printed for permanent record of system usage.

There is considerable interest in ETVs by electronics manufacturers. They are an especially important material transport device for those companies concerned about work-in-progress inventory. Reduction of inventory can be achieved through improved process flow control and reduced batch sizes. This results in an increase in the total number of moves between operations to maintain the same or higher levels of finished good unit shipments. However, reduced batch sizes means lower weights and volumes, making the use of ETVs feasible. The ETVs also support asynchronous-type processing, helping to reduce work-in-progress.

In summary:

An overhead AGV system can provide the flexibility of a floor AGV system at a lower cost. It is faster, simpler, and keeps the work floor free of obstructions. However, future layout changes are more involved and more expensive than with a floor AGV system. It is, however, an important alternative to consider when selecting a material-handling conveying system.

Chapter Twelve

AGVs in material handling

The first AGV application was for transporting groceries in warehouses. To date, they are still used as an integral part of automated material-handling and storage, whether it be in a warehouse, distribution centre, or automated factory environment. They can readily be synchronised with other material-handling devices, such as AS/RS. They permit system accountability by tracking material with accurate real-time response. AGVs also provide delivery confirmation which can help eliminate misplaced matcrials or late delivery. This supports just-in-time concepts, thus reducing both floor stock and inventory, which in turn increases available floor-space for production. AGVs are also suitable for handling fragile and/or valuable materials that require gentle and/or precise handling. Material damage is usually substantially reduced because of automatic loading and unloading, automatic avoidance and collision control, and controlled accelerations and decelerations. Experience has proven that AGVs in material-handling applications are a key to both manufacturing and warehousing efficiency.

Material handling has a broad range of applicatioins as indicated in the general case study section of this chapter. The vehicles used may be tuggers with trailers, pallet trucks, high-lift trucks, or unit load carriers. The specific case history section of this chapter contains four examples of applications, one for each type of vehicle.

Special considerations
The specific material-handling requirements of a given facility must first be assessed. For example, the postal service might

require the movement of several tons of mail through its facility within a few hours, warehousing or distribution centres might require mass storage of material in large high-rise systems, and a manufacturing environment might require just-in-time inventory control whereby only the right amount of material is delivered at just the time of need.

Several factors should be considered when designing an AGV system for any material-handling situation. First, the system should be flexible to accommodate future requirements, both foreseen and unforeseen. This includes such factors as changes in load size or configuration, throughput requirements, and the ability to interface with other future automation. Secondly, the system should be modular to accommodate changes in product mix or in the product itself. (Some suppliers are offering vehicles with interchangeable work platforms as shown in Fig. 12.1.) The third factor is to design and consider the complete material-handling system as a whole unit so that effective integration is possible. Although only one small segment may be installed at any one time, it must be able to be integrated into the whole material-handling scheme.

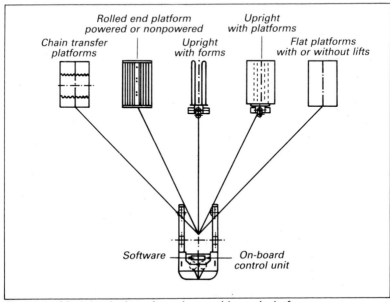

Fig. 12.1 Modular design – interchangeable work platforms

Whereas AGV systems seem to be readily accepted by the work-force in manufacturing and assembly operations, there seems to be some reluctance for acceptance in strictly material-handling applications. Many material handlers, such as fork-truck drivers, see these systems as a direct threat to their jobs. To help alleviate such problems and to promote acceptance of the system, the workers need to be made aware of all aspects of the system and how it will affect their jobs. If they understand their relationship with the system they will no longer see it as a threat and acceptance will be much greater.

In terms of the guidepath layout, some specific considerations need to be kept in mind. If at all possible, aisle space permitting, bidirectional travel on a given path should be avoided since it will reduce the system efficiency as vehicles wait for a clear path before proceeding. If bidirectional travel is necessary on a long stretch, spurs should be incorporated to permit passing, as shown in Fig. 12.2a. Spurs should also be provided to avoid congestion along the

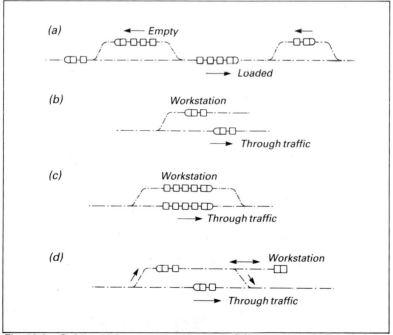

Fig. 12.2   Guidepath layout considerations: (a) spurs along bidirectional path, (b) dead-end spur, (c) continuous spur, and (d) continuous spur-containing dead end

main guidepath at load and unload stations. Spurs can either be dead-ended, as shown in Fig. 12.2b, or continuous, as shown in Fig. 12.2c and d. The spurs shown in Fig. 12.2b and d require a vehicle with reversing capabilities and would be mainly limited to fork-type vehicles or unit load carriers. The continuous spur, as shown in Fig. 12.2c, would be ideal for a tugger system.

The number of vehicles required in a system depends on several factors, notably: running time, blocking time, idle time, load/unload time, charging time, repair and maintenance time, distance travelled, average velocity, acceleration and deceleration times, layout. Simulation is the only way to obtain a realistic insight as to the number of vehicles required; however, a rough estimate can quickly be made as follows:[2]

1. Determine average trip time (TT) in minutes:

$$TT = \frac{D}{V} + LT$$

where D is the average distance the AGV travels per trip (metres), V is the vehicle speed (m/min), and LT is the load/unload time (min).

2. Determine theoretical number of vehicles:

$$\text{No. of vehicles} = \frac{\text{Required load movements per min}}{\text{Loads/trip (for a vehicle)}} \times TT$$

3. Determine actual number of vehicles by dividing by an efficiency factor:

$$\text{Actual no. of vehicles} = \frac{\text{No. of vehicles}}{\text{Efficiency factor}}$$

The efficiency factor needs to account for blocking time, idle time, charging time, repair time and other factors that influence the system efficiency. A reasonable estimate may be between 70 and 85% efficiency.

For example, if the average distance is 1400m, vehicle velocity is 60m/min, load and unload is 4min, required load movements/min is 2.4 (144 per hour), loads for each vehicle per trip is 8, and the system efficiency is estimated to be 75%, the resultant number of vehicles is:

$$TT = \frac{1400}{60} + 4 = 27.33$$

$$\text{No. of vehicles} = \frac{2.4}{8} \times 27.33 = 8.2$$

$$\text{Actual no. of vehicles} = \frac{8.2}{0.75} = 10.9 \text{ (i.e. 11 vehicles)}$$

The type of vehicle selected for the system is dependent upon the application requirements. For applications where large volumes of material need to be transported over long distances with relatively few stops, the logical choice is a tugger system hauling several trailers. The trailer design is dependent upon aisle and intersection widths (see Chapter Four). Applications involving medium to moderately long distances, with moderate volume rates and with more stops, call for fork-style trucks. Where the lift does not exceed 40in. (approx. 1m), pallet trucks are suitable. For those applications requiring lifts of up to 20ft (approx. 6m), high-lift trucks are required. Special versions of this type of AGV include side-load and counterbalance reach trucks. Typically, all pallet trucks can lift loads on skids or pallets directly off the floor. Unit load vehicles are used in applications that have relatively short to medium distances, with moderate volumes and with a large number of stops. The major advantage of this type of vehicle is its high degree of manoeuvrability and its compactness. There are a variety of deck designs, such as passive or powered roller conveyor, belt conveyor, and lift/lower deck, which allow interfacing with almost all conveying systems.

General case studies

There are numerous applications of AGVs in material-handling environments. This section presents a general overview of the range of these applications and the following section discusses four specific applications in greater detail.

A grocery wholesaler expanded its operation by adding a second building 250ft (approx. 75m) away. This presented shipping and receiving operational problems, as well as inventory control problems. Thus, a tunnel was built between the facilities and an AGV system was installed. All receiving is performed in one facility, shipping from the other, and order picking coordinated between them. The AGV system consists of three tractors, each pulling six 4000lb (approx. 1800kg) capacity trailers.[11]

An office furniture manufacturer uses a six-vehicle AGV system to transport materials from the AS/RS output conveyors to workstations and to provide inter-department transportation between workstations. Each tractor tows a train of non-powered roller-bed trailers. An operator can easily transfer loads from the trailers to match non-powered floor stands.[11]

A major aircraft rework facility had the problem of transporting rebuilt and new parts to many locations within a large facility. The solution was provided by 12 unit load vehicles capable of automatically picking up 36 × 48in. tote trays full of parts from the disassembly areas and delivering the parts to the respective rebuild shops.[11]

A cosmetic manufacturer increased its manufacturing and warehousing facility floor area by nearly 50% with the addition of a new warehouse. The warehouse was designed so that it could be converted to manufacturing space if needed in the future. The handling system selected included 28 narrow-aisle pallet trucks to move the raw material and finished goods. The AGV system is integrated with 14 automatic pick-up and delivery stations. Inventory accuracy provided by the system has eliminated the need for the biannual manual inventory, saving approximately 280–400 man-days per year.[11]

An outboard motor manufacturer needed a means of speeding up material handling within segments of its manufacturing plant to improve its productivity. The plant rearranged its assembly lines and streamlined material flow through the facility to eliminate the need for a work-in-progress holding area. The material-handling (AGV) system selected comprised three floor-to-floor pallet trucks and one tugger unit. The 4200ft (approx. 1280m) guidepath contains ten stops for the pallet trucks and five stops for the tugger. The results have brought about a more timely delivery of parts and a 50% reduction in the amount of inventory required.[12]

At a milk homogenisation plant, eight AGV unit load vehicles, capable of carrying two independently controlled pallets, transport the pallets from a production station into a storage and retrieval area. From here the products are transported by AGVs to an order-picking area or directly to shipping. Each vehicle positions itself at a loading conveyor and raises its own powered roller bed to meet the full pallets for loading or unloading. The pallets are monitored by the central computer for inventory and production control.

These six case studies give an indication of the variety of industries using AGV systems. The automotive industry is one of the largest users, as the following case studies will show. There are also a multitude of non-manufacturing applications, such as in hospitals and offices (Chapter Sixteen is devoted to such applications).

Specific case studies

GM-BOC – Willow Run Plant*

At the end of the 1981 model year, the GM-BOC Willow Run Plant was experiencing an exorbitant average monthly inventory balance. The transportation mode was therefore changed in several instances from rail to truck, thus decreasing in-transit days by 34. Although this reduced the inventory balance, the already over-burdened truck receiving systems became saturated (the truck volume increased from a total of 140–160 trucks per day).

While the rail docks were centrally located, the main truck receiving dock was located in one corner of the plant and the trim shop, which uses 65% of the truck receipts, was located in the opposite corner. Owing to the massively congested conditions in the truck dock, parts were being damaged and lost, and were failing to reach the point of operation on time. The average round trip from the truck dock to the trim shop was 4600ft (approx. 1400m), which limited drivers to about three trips per hour.

It was decided that an AGV system would solve these problems without requiring more manpower. The payback projection, based on transportation savings, reduced parts damage and some labour savings, was less than 6 months when converted to net cash flow. A tugger system (supplied by Control Engineering Company, an affiliate of Jervis B. Webb Company) was selected since large volumes had to be moved over a long distance. Since 80% of the proposed guidepath was over a wood-block floor, it was decided to build a 5ft (approx. 1.5m) wide concrete path adjacent to, but separate from, the existing aisles. By October 1983 the system was operational and accepted by the plant.

The vehicles are loaded and programmed at the main dock and

---

* This case study is based on a presentation by Robert L. Wells, Superintendent of Material Management, BOC Group of GM at Willow Run, Michigan.

have the capacity to deliver up to 120 tons (approx. 110,000kg) of material to the trim shop and chassis department, which is adjacent to the main dock. Each vehicle has two 12 × 4ft (approx. 3.6 × 1.2m) ball-hitched self-trailing trailers which are loaded with straight rack or skid loads and sent exclusively to one of 17 predetermined stops. Usually, a trailer is unloaded at its destination by the stockman responsible for that area, and if prior approval is given, he returns the empty containers on an empty train. This has provided the additional benefit of reducing the number of empty containers that accumulate in dead-end aisles.

A vehicle can be programmed to take the shortest of three routes to any predetermined stop, and on its return trip, if the battery is 80% discharged, the vehicle will automatically go into the battery spur for recharging (charging is usually required after approximately four 8-hour shifts). The vehicle movements are monitored at the receiving office and if the vehicle does not reach its next zone within a predetermined time, a signal is given which alerts the receiving check. The material supervisor for that area is then called upon to check the status of the vehicle.

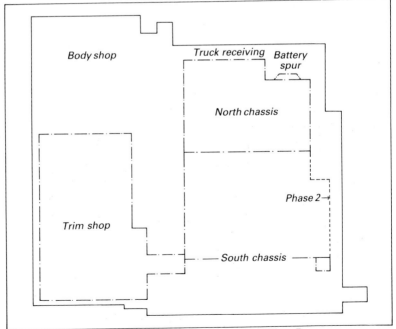

Fig. 12.3   Original guidepath layout at GM-BOC Willow Run

As with most new equipment, some teething problems caused system inefficiency. However, the ease of modification of AGV systems allowed these problems to be corrected quickly. For example, bidirectional guidepath zones were eliminated by adding an additional guidepath, as indicated by the dotted line in Fig. 12.3; in addition, vehicles were prevented from standing idle for long periods of time by signalling the stockman upon the train's arrival.

Some of the major benefits experienced included less fork-truck damage to skids, less mutilation of skids and parts in general, elimination of misrouted and foreign parts in the serviced areas, and the return of empty containers. The back-log of material on the truck dock has also been eliminated and the amount of overtime worked by material handlers has been greatly reduced. Finally, the plant's average monthly inventory balance has been cut in half and the demurrage and detention costs have been reduced to zero, since the trucks can be unloaded immediately.

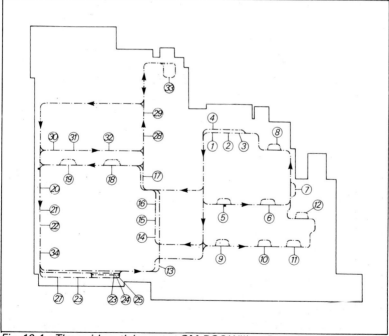

Fig. 12.4   The guidepath layout at GM-BOC Willow Run after expansion (numbers represent stopping points)

Owing to the success of the original system, an additional 4500ft (approx 1400m) of guidepath (see Fig. 12.4), 15 new vehicles, and 12 new unloading spurs were added in late 1985. This addition enhanced the material-handling capabilities, allowed much greater flexibility than before, and incorporated the body shop and the salvage area for the first time. The 12 new unloading spurs allow an almost obstacle-free flow of vehicles through the plant. A new trim truck dock has been built next to the trim shop which eliminates the long, across-the-plant runs that were previously required, and permits even more of the rail transportation to be converted to trucks.

Whereas the original system consisted of eight Prontow Model 01 tuggers, each with a pulling capacity of 30,000lb (approx. 13,500kg), the new vehicles are Prontow Model 1000 (Fig. 12.5) with pulling capacities of 50,000lb (approx. 22,500kg). The vehicles may be used both in manual and automatic modes: when in the manual mode, the AGV may be placed over the guidepath wire and released to operate automatically; when in the automatic mode, it can only be placed in a manual mode by means of a key switch. (The vehicle cannot be driven manually when it is locked in the automatic mode.)

Fig. 12.5   The Prontow Model 1000 tugger vehicle

GM-BOC – Orion Plant*

The Orion Plant, a 3.7 million ft^2 (approx. 350,000m^2) assembly plant, has always used just-in-time inventory control system as the normal method of material handling. The use of AGVs to pick up loads at a receiving dock and deliver them directly to their point of use on the assembly line, is an important part of Orions's goal of just-in-time delivery.

Traditional US auto manufacturers receive about 75% of their parts by rail, and about 25% by truck. The BOC Orion Plant had to change this approach in order to get more timely shipments from the vendors. Since railway lines are usually much closer to production areas than receiving docks, railway lines can be installed inside the plant, adjacent to the assembly line. Trucks, on the other hand, do not usually enter the plant but are unloaded at exterior docks. The parts are then transported over rather long delivery lines to the manufacturing area.

The 22 AGVs, manufactured by Conco-Tellus, give this facility a reliable, cost-effective way to supply assemblers with parts from the dock. They are able to transport approximately 70% of the incoming stock to the line by automatically picking up a variety of part containers, and taking them to the 69 different 'drop zones' in the trim and chassis departments.

Two of the vehicles in the system are high-lift models, capable of stacking 6000lb (approx. 2700kg) loads to heights of 12ft (approx. 3.7m). The other 20 vehicles can be converted to high-lift models by attaching high-lift masts. The high-lift vehicles deliver containers of front wheel hubs to two-level flow-through racks at the assembly line, and deposit loads in the upper level. The containers flow by gravity to a lift at the opposite end (Fig. 12.6) which lowers the container to floor level, and an assembler removes the hubs from the container and attaches them to the cars on the assembly line. When the container is empty, the assembler presses a button so that the empty container is sent down to the bottom level of the rack and is picked up by the next available AGV which returns it to the receiving dock.

Orion's AGV system contains 24,000ft (approx. 7300m) of guidepath in the chassis and trim departments (Fig. 12.7). Vehicles are dispatched by an operator at the dock, using a CRT/keyboard terminal. (There are plans to bar-code dispatching

---

* This case study was written by Thomas J. Harris, Material Coordinator, Material Department, BOC Orion Plant, Michigan.

Fig. 12.6   High-lift truck at GM-BOC Orion

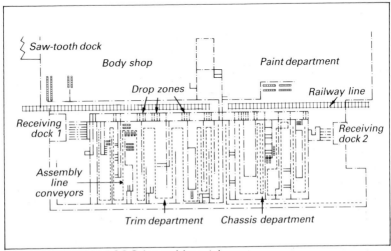

Fig. 12.7   The GM-BOC Orion guidepath layout

in the future.) Vehicles can be summoned to a pick-up zone to deliver empty containers to the dock by using a key-operated 'call button' in each zone.

The control system consists of a mainframe computer with an identical back-up, which is also utilised by the truck repair group for record keeping. All vehicles in the system have on-board microcomputers and an FM radio link is used for communication between the control system and the vehicles.

A vehicle will automatically move to the battery room when 80% of its battery's capacity has been used (typically after 8 hours of continuous operation).

Photocells inside each vehicle's straddle arms are used to align the vehicles for load pick-up. Photocells located in the tips of each fork are used for alignment of the fork with the fork pockets of the various containers used at the plant.

The AGV system has been designed so that the vehicles can move off and return to the guidepath automatically. In this mode of operation, the vehicle's on-board intelligence controls the movement of the vehicle while still communicating, via FM link, with the central control. This feature allows flexibility in the system, as well as the ability to make test changes in the guidepath prior to actual guidepath alterations being made.

It is intended to make further enhancements to Orion's AGV system by including photocells in the floor at the drop zones to notify the CRT operator of full zones, so that material can be routed to another drop zone or held on the dock until the full zone is cleared. It is also planned to incorporate additional over and under automatic stocking. On-board vehicle control panels are currently being replaced to provide instant vehicle diagnostics for plant maintenance personnel.

With Orion's just-in-time goals for material handling and the heavy volume of truck shipments necessary to accomplish this goal, the AGV system has been a very welcome asset.

GM-CPC – Bay City Plant*

The plant is responsible for making nearly 300 different types of transmission valves with a production rate of approximately 370,000 units per day. In the past, many material-handling

---

* This case study is based on information and material provided by Ron Scheall, Industrial Engineer with the CPC Plant located at Bay City, Michigan. He was the project engineer responsible for the system from its inception.

problems were experienced, such as stock being sent to wrong destinations, incorrect part identificatin due to human error, lack of inventory control at intermediate operations, and excessive time spent locating and handling stock. Owing to errors in inventory control, shipping deadlines were missed, excessive stock was sometimes generated, and raw material shortages were occasionally experienced. Also, the inability to schedule optimum lot sizes of a given part caused excessive changeovers adversely affecting machine utilisation.

Since there are many different part routings, it made it very difficult to control inventory and part flow in a manual systematic manner. For these reasons, it was determined that the best solution to these problems was an automatic computer-controlled material-handling storage and inventory system. An AGV system, used in conjuction with an AS/RS, was therefore selected. Parts are generated at the automatic bar machine, transferred by AGVs to the wash operations, and then to the storage area. From there, AGVs transport the parts in baskets to all subsequent operations,· such as miscellaneous secondary machining, heat-treat, in-feed grind, through-feed grind, and inspection.

Parts are manufactured on automatic screw machines and collected in baskets. As the machine operators collect a number of baskets, they will call for an AGV to pick up and transport them to the wash area. The baskets are automatically unloaded, passed through the wash and presented to the audit operators. At this station, the part is positively identified through the use of computer vision, while the basket is identified by a bar-code reader. The part identification is determined at subsequent operations by determining the basket identity. Parts are then transported by the AGVs to the AS/RS to await further processing. The baskets are identified and weighed to give an exact part count and are then stored. This system is used to maintain control of in-process inventory. Whenever material is returned to the AS/RS from any operation, such as miscellaneous machining or heat-treat, baskets of stock are re-identified to ensure that the process operation has been completed and this information is entered into the control system.

The AGV system consists of 14 wire-guided unit load vehicles (Model 140 Unicar), supplied by Barrett. The deck consists of powered roller conveyors for transferring the baskets to and from the load/unload stations. Typically the vehicles carry nine baskets per trip. Fig. 12.8 shows a vehicle transferring a load at one of the

Fig. 12.8   The GM-BOC Bay City unit load carrier

stations. Most stations transfer all nine baskets from the three parallel conveyors at a given stop; however, some stops have only single conveyor lines transferring only three baskets from one of the parallel conveyors.

The wire guidepath, shown in Fig. 12.9, is over 7000ft long (approx. 2130m) and has essentially been broken into two systems. The first consists of three vehicles which transfer baskets of parts from the automatic bar machines to the wash and identification area (because coolants and oils drip onto the vehicles from the baskets before they and the parts are washed, it was decided to use only three instead of all 14 vehicles). The remaining 11 vehicles are used on the rest of the system to transport the baskets of parts to the various operations. The two systems overlap at the empty basket storage area. The main vehicle system returns washed empty baskets to be reused while the three-vehicle system picks up baskets at the same station and delivers them to the automatic bar machines.

Although many of the original material-handling objectives have been realised, some have not. It is difficult to make a judgement in some areas since, between the time the system was started and its completion, some product changes were experienced, nullifying some of the projected benefits. Probably one of

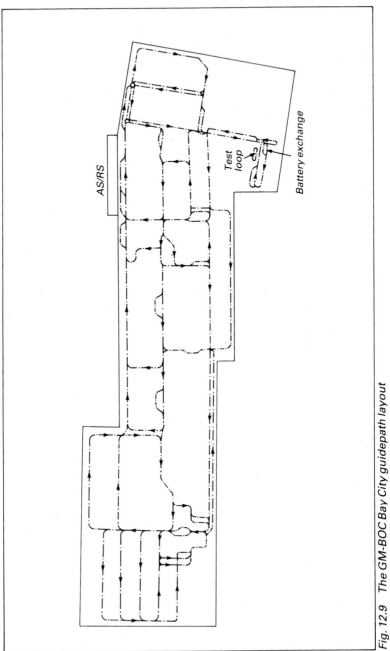

Fig. 12.9 The GM-BOC Bay City guidepath layout

the major benefits, however, is the complete inventory control achieved over work-in-progress parts. It is now possible to make intelligent decisions when determining whether to change machine set-ups or continue with the present part. By knowing the exact quantities of both the parts on hand and the number required, it can be determined whether present production should be continued or whether the machine should be shut down and a changeover in tooling made. Previously it was an educated guess.

Steelcase – Kentwood Physical Distribution Center*

Steelcase is a leading manufacturer of office furniture. It currently has over 8 million ft^2 (approx. 740,000m^2) in its manufacturing complex in Grand Rapids, Michigan. Production began in 1983 in the first three buildings of a planned 6 million ft^2 (approx. 560,000m^2) manufacturing complex, projected for completion in 1993. A Conco-Tellus AGV pallet-truck system was selected for use in the Physical Distribution Center and is currently utilised to transport loaded carts from the packaging area on the second floor of that building to an elevator that goes to the staging and loading area on the first floor. Fig. 12.10 illustrates the floor and the 1000ft long (approx. 3000m) guidepath layout.

Steelcase shipping personnel receive packaged goods and load transport carts at either of the two packing lanes within the Distribution Center. Staff at each packing lane fill up to six carts per hour, giving a total number filled of 12 per hour. When a cart is full, the worker pushes it into position to be picked up by the AGV pallet trucks. Each packing lane has two pick-up zones, each capable of holding four full carts. Empty carts are placed in the centre zone by the AGVs. Photocells in the floor detect both full and open cart positions, relaying that information to the system controller for vehicle dispatch.

Package racks (carts) used in the AGV system were designed with a platform size and height matching similar racks used in the electrified powered monorail system, and were also designed with castor wheels to permit manual movement. They are confined to the building, and transport packaged products from the second floor packaging area to the first floor shipping facility. An undercarriage (fork pockets) was designed into the carts so that the AGVs could handle unbalanced loads.

---

* This case study is based on information provided by Gerry Albers, Material Handling Engineer, Physical Distribution, Steelcase Inc., Grand Rapids, Michigan.

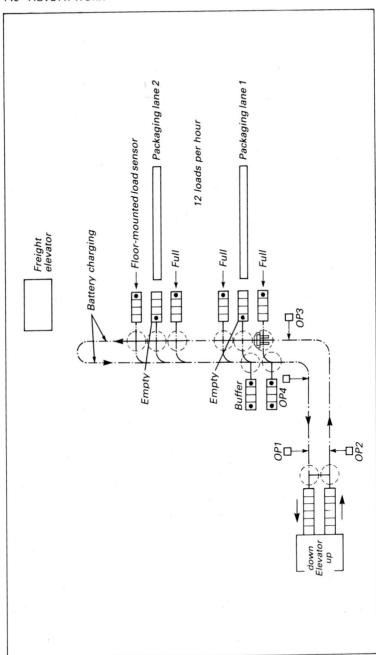

Fig. 12.10 Guidepath layour, Steelcase Kentwood Plant

Full carts are delivered to the vertical 'down' elevator and empty carts are received from the 'up' elevator. The elevator transfer mechanism that receives or delivers carts to the AGV is about 18in. (approx. 46cm) above floor level, well within the 60in. (approx. 152cm) lifting height capability of the vehicles. Empty carts are taken from the elevator to the empty cart zone either in packing lane 1 or 2. An immediate floor buffer area is also provided for both full and empty racks. This buffer has two lanes with room for eight carts in each lane, and is only used when empty carts cannot be transported to their normal zones or full carts cannot be transported down by the elevator.

Communication with the external computer system is through an optical transmission device. Since the storage of the on-board control computer memorises information from the stationary control system, a vehicle can operate without the need of continuous computer transmission.

The system was designed with capacity for future expansion, both in production (increased throughput) and advanced controls implementation. Even as installed, the two vehicle system has capacity to expand its functional capability. System longevity has been guaranteed by an enhanced ability to adapt to changing production methods and layout changes.

There have been no operator/employee acceptance problems, and in general the system has performed as expected. Conservative figures show a payback period in terms of labour savings of 3.5 years. The system was installed with the capacity to handle additional production volume without immediately requiring additional vehicles or system controls.

Employees exercise care when positioning racks at pick-up points, thereby eliminating the problem of roll-away due to castor lead (all four rack castors can swivel) or uneven floors. This provides a dependable interface between the rack and AGV, and eliminates the need for special rack positioning fixtures. Proper handling of these same racks by fork-truck drivers in the loading and staging areas also eliminates potential damage to the bottom fork pocket bar. Application of these handling methods ensures reliable and productive operation of the AGV system.

In summary:

Material handling was the original and is still the most common application area for AGVs. This is primarily due to their flexibility, ease of system modification, ability to interface with other material-handling automation (such as AS/RS), improved material tracking and inventory control, and the ability to reduce part damage and to handle fragile material.

There are several special considerations that particularly apply to material-handling environments: the labour force, for various reasons, does not accept AGVs as readily for material-handling as for other applications; and the guidepath layout considerations are somewhat different from those for assembly operations (as is the number of vehicles required for a system). required for a system).

The case studies show a wide range of material-handling applications using AGVs, as well as the type of vehicles used. The specific case studies show the type of applications for each of the various types of vehicle.

The case studies give a general overview of the range of material-handling applications using AGVs, as well as the type of vehicles used. Four specific industrial applications are also discussed in greater detail.

Chapter Thirteen

AGVs in assembly

In addition to material-handling operations, AGV systems are increasingly being used for assembly processes. The number of vehicles required, however, is often significantly greater; some plants may involve the use of hundreds of vehicles in a single line, whereas a large material-handling system may involve only 20–30 vehicles. The asynchronous capability of AGVs make their use particularly attractive in assembly of items that have large option contents. By providing great flexibility in designing an assembly process, increased productivity and quality can be realised. This chapter presents some of the techniques and options to be considered while planning a new system layout, followed by several case studies.

Special considerations

Instead of being restricted to serial-type (synchronous) assembly processes, AGVs afford the opportunity to use work islands. A work island is a group of at least two workstations at which operators are performing similar work. All major components to be assembled can be kitted in tote trays at a central parts-processing area and carried to the work islands by the AGVs. Only small parts and fasteners should be provided at the work island, as well as the necessary tools. The vehicles carry the required parts from a central parts area, thus greatly reducing the amount of material handling and non-value-added work content.

There are two major approaches to AGV assembly. The first involves attaching the workpiece to the AGV and having all assembly, testing, and inspection performed while the work remains on the vehicle as it moves from station to station. The AGV acts much like a traditional conveyor system and also requires a considerable number of vehicles. The second approach, referred to as 'stop and drop', is to use vehicles only to move the workpiece from one workstation to another. When the workpiece is completed, a vehicle picks it up and delivers it to the next operation. It is estimated that for larger systems this method could cut the number of vehicles required in half. On the other hand, this method also requires a longer cycle time at each workstation and idle time for the workstation operators, thus decreasing the throughput. It also reduces the ability to use opportunity charging. Another consideration is that special transfer mechanisms may be required at each workstation to permit loading and unloading of the workpieces.

The layout of typical work islands is shown in Fig. 13.1. There are many advantages to such a system. Firstly, if production demand decreases, this can be accommodated by deactivating some of the parallel workstations. Likewise, if demand exceeds the capability of the present system, it is possible that more parallel workstations may be added if floor-space permits. Another advantage is that workers can hold the vehicle in the workstation for the amount of time necessary to do the job right. If

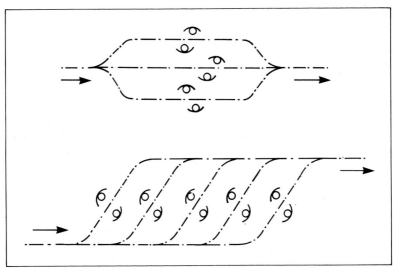

Fig. 13.1   Work island layout

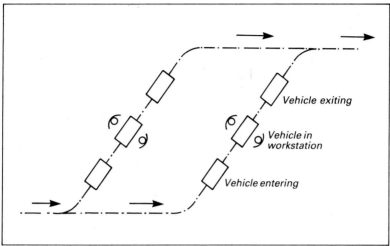

Fig. 13.2   Three vehicle positions in parallel workstation path

trouble is experienced, workers are often able to deal with it if they are given a little extra time. This also permits the workers to do their own inspection, sometimes eliminating the need for direct inspectors. Many workstations consist of two or more operators, and team-work tends to promote pride and cooperation among the team members.

To minimise idle time for the workstation operators, a vehicle carrying a workpiece should always be ready to move into the station. Also, it is important to ensure that the vehicle carrying the finished assembly is able to leave on command and not be delayed because of traffic-control delays. The parallel guidepath should be of sufficient length to hold one vehicle leaving the workstation, one in the workstation, and another entering (Fig. 13.2).

Most systems require some method of re-sequencing the AGVs back into their original sequence. Whenever an asynchronous system interfaces with a synchronous line, re-sequencing is required to match the sequence of the synchronous line. Another situation that could require re-sequencing is when the AGV needs to return to the parts provision area between workstations to obtain another tote tray of kitted parts. The kitted tote trays are usually made up from the manifests which are in the original sequence. Either the vehicles must be re-sequenced or the tote trays sequenced to match the new sequence of the vehicles arriving at the parts area. The re-sequencing of AGVs is usually

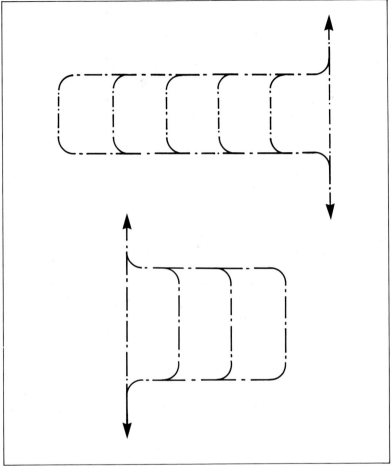

Fig. 13.3 Re-sequencing loops

accomplished in a re-sequencing loop or job buffer, where the vehicles are held until they can be released in sequence (Fig. 13.3). The size of the re-sequencing loop is determined by how far out of sequence the vehicle can get (the type of information simulation will provide).

A system needs to be well thought out and designed to be able to take full advantage of all the benefits that an AGV assembly system can offer. If a product experiences much change or has any amount of option content, the flexibility offered by AGV system assembly appears to be well worth the effort.

Case studies

GM-BOC Lansing – chassis and engine merge

When the GM-BOC Lansing Plants were renovated, it was decided to investigate alternatives to the standard monorail systems used in the past. After determining the process requirements for the chassis and engine merge, a comparison of the available conveyance methods was made. Out of five possible methods, AGVs received the top ranking. The factors considered in the evaluation included process flexibility, facility cost, operating manpower requirements, maintenance, work area accessibility, buffer ability between systems, system rearrangement flexibility, and system complexity.

The chassis-merge line and the engine-stuff line are two separate systems. The chassis-merge line comprises about 1200ft (approx. 365m) of guidepath, 32 AGVs, and a total of 13 workstations (Fig. 13.4). The engine-merge line consists of about 300ft (approx. 90m) of guidepath and 12 AGVs (Fig. 13.5). While the basic vehicles on both lines are identical (Eaton-Kenway AGVs), the vehicle work platforms contain different fixturing to accommodate each application.

The chassis-merge process (Fig. 13.4) begins with the rear axle subassembly and front steering knuckles being loaded onto an AGV. The rear axle subassembly is loaded manually while the front steering knuckle is loaded by robot. The vehicle proceeds to the exhaust pipe assembly loading station where a one-piece welded exhaust system is loaded. The vehicle again proceeds, this

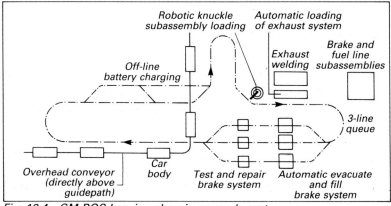

Fig. 13.4 GM-BOC Lansing chassis-merge layout

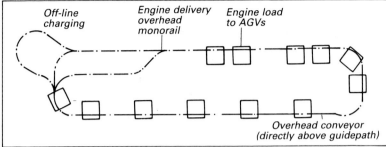

Fig. 13.5 *GM-BOC Lansing engine-merge layout*

time to the brake-line station where preassembled brake and fuel lines are loaded into the fixturing. The brake lines are then connected to the rear axle and front knuckles, and the vehicle is released to move to one of three parallel paths where the brake system is automatically evacuated and filled with brake fluid as shown in Fig. 13.6. After completion, the vehicle moves to the test and repair station where the brake system is pressure tested for leaks. Sufficient time is provided by use of the parallel paths to allow an operator to locate leaks and repair them. In all manual loading stations and workstations the operator has control over the vehicle release.

Fig. 13.6 *GM-BOC Lansing AGVs at brake evacuate and fill station*

The vehicles containing the completed chassis components exit the test and repair area and remain in a queue until they are released to meet the main synchronous overhead conveyor that carries the car bodies. When a car body arrives, the AGV system controller will release the AGV that contains the appropriate matching chassis. (Two models are built on this line.) The released AGV travels directly underneath and parallel to the overhead body conveyor, aligning itself under and tracking the continuously moving body. This is accomplished by the AGV utilising a reflected light beam from a target (reflector) mounted on the overhead conveyor body carrier. After the AGV becomes synchronised with the conveyor, the operator activates the AGV lift table (work platform) to raise the chassis components into place under the body. Personnel fasten the components in place, and the vehicle returns to its starting point.

Engines arrive at the engine-merge area from the engine plant by means of a monorail. An operator starts the engine-merge process (Fig. 13.5) by removing the engine from the monorail and putting it on the AGV. The vehicle proceeds to the merge point where it awaits release by the main controller. As with the

Fig. 13.7 GM-BOC Lansing engine-merge AGV

chassis-merge operation, the engine-merge AGV synchronises itself with the overhead body carrier. Again, an operator activates the lift table to insert the engine and transaxle into the body from underneath (Fig. 13.7). Personnel then fasten the engine and transaxle assembly into place, and the vehicle returns to receive another engine.

In both the chassis- and engine-merge lines, the vehicles operate on opportunity charging at each workstation. However, if any vehicle does not receive sufficient charge through this method, it can leave the main line before starting its cycle and receive off-line charging (Figs. 13.4 and 13.5).

Benefits from these two AGV systems have been apparent. A comparison of the end-of-line brake-repair rates obtained by the AGV system shows that less than one-sixth of the repairs are required, compared with the rates obtained by the previous monorail system. Much of this improved quality is attributed to the test and repair station capabilities offered by the AGV system. Another advantage offered by this system is that the brake fill and test equipment is now stationary, whereas in the former system it was suspended above the monorail line and travelled with it. This has reduced the maintenance service calls on this equipment by a factor of 2.8. Other benefits are expected to become evident as more experience is gained on the systems.

GM-BOC Lansing – engine dress

The Lansing Engine Dress Plant is responsible for preparing and delivering engines to keep the two chassis assembly plants operational. Since two synchronous monorail systems for engine dress were already operational in the plant from the previous model production, it was more difficult to justify the cost of a new AGV system. However, after careful consideration of such factors as increased quality, ergonomics, productivity, and flexibility, together with the cost, it was determined that the AGV system could be justified.

The engine-dress line has been designed to produce 140 engines per hour to meet the production rate of the two chassis assembly plants. It consists of about 7500ft (approx. 2290m) of guidepath, 95 Schindler-Digitron AGVs obtained through Eaton-Kenway, and a total of 40 workstations grouped into nine work islands (Fig. 13.8). Each work island consists of two or more parallel workstations with each workstation manned by one or two

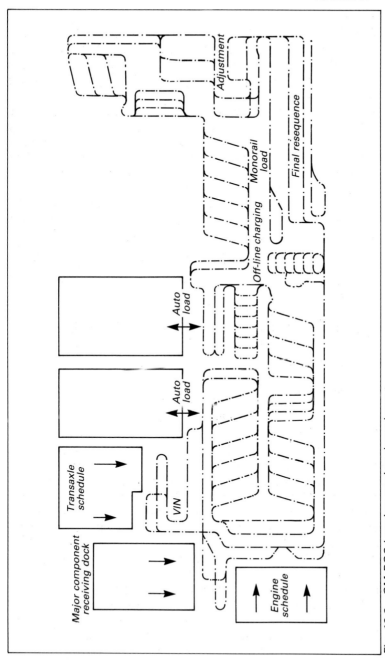

Fig. 13.8 GM-BOC Lansing engine-dress layout

Fig. 13.9   GM-BOC Lansing AGV at engine assembly workstation

operators (Fig. 13.9). The workstations provide the operators with the necessary tools, fasteners, and a few small parts. Other necessary parts are kitted in tote trays which are placed on the AGV by robots in the parts-provisioning areas.

At the beginning of the engine-dress process, an operator using a CRT/keyboard terminal and a hand-held bar-code scanner, inputs the line sequence number and option code for the next engine entering the AGV control system. Through use of the option code, the system controller can identify which engine is on which AGV. Since the option code contains such information as the engine type, transaxle type, and option content (engine block heater and air conditioning), the expected assembly time and optimum lift height for assembly can be controlled at each workstation.

The operator loads the engine onto the AGV and then manually releases it to the transaxle station. The transaxle station consists of two parallel lines where the transaxles are loaded onto the AGV and then assembled to the engine. Again from the station the AGVs are manually released. From all the remaining workstations in the system, the vehicles are automatically released by the system controller.

After transaxle load, each vehicle travels to the 'VIN' station where a robot laser etches the vehicle identification number (VIN) on the engine. While at these first three workstations, the AGVs remain in their original input sequence and are now ready to move into the first of two parts-provisioning areas. Here a robot loads each AGV with a tote tray containing the appropriate manually preselected parts in a kit form. The kits contain all the parts necessary for the next three workstations for the specific engine on the AGV.

Prior to entry into each workstation, the vehicle adjusts its lift table to the preprogrammed height; however, the operator can override the lift by pressing a vehicle switch. The vehicles are typically programmed to remain in the workstations for 90 to 140 seconds, depending on the option content. Ten seconds before the programmed automatic release, a warning light is activated and either workstation operator has the ability to hold the vehicle for more time, if necessary, to complete his/her work or to do minor repairs. Once the vehicle is held beyond its automatic release time, a red light will alert the supervisor of the problem. If the problem is too time-consuming or difficult to repair in the workstation, a 'send to repair' button on the vehicle is activated. This will divert the vehicle to a rework station at the end of the system.

After completing these three workstations, the vehicles are guided to the second parts-provisioning area where a robot removes the first tote tray and then loads the next one. Since the tote trays are kitted according to the original sequence, and the AGVs are now out of sequence (because of varying times at the workstations), the AGVs are sent through a re-sequencing buffer. (There is consideration being given to redesign the robot workcell so that the robot can select and load the proper tote tray without having to re-sequence the vehicles.)

After receiving the second tote tray, the AGV proceeds through the next three assembly workstations. The vehicle then stops at the electrical test-stations where the engine's electrical components and wiring are checked. Outside this one station there are no direct inspectors, and inspection is performed by the workstation operators prior to vehicle release. If the send to repair button has been activated, the vehicle will automatically enter the rework station where only two people are needed to meet repair demands. Otherwise, the AGV proceeds to either one of the two off-load stations, depending on which chassis assembly plant the engine is to be sent to. An overhead monorail carries the engines between the engine plant and the two chassis assembly plants. Since the engines are out of sequence again, they are re-sequenced manually, using an overhead power and free conveyor system. The power and free conveyor also acts as a buffer.

As with the chassis- and engine-merge systems, the engine-dress system is designed to operate on opportunity charging. If there is not sufficient charge, the vehicle is re-routed through the charging area before starting its next cycle. The entire engine-dress cycle requires approximately 35–40min depending on the engine options.

There seems to be considerable satisfaction with the system and its operation. Some of the benefits realised over the previous overhead monorail conveyor are: the amount of walk time and stock time required has been reduced, giving the operators more productive time; it is easier to balance the time, due to varying option content; reduced absenteeism rate is experienced; the number of repair personnel has been reduced considerably; no direct inspectors are required; and the product quality has significantly improved. There have been other benefits, but they are harder to quantify.

Finally, there seems to be a considerable difference in the workers' attitudes compared to typical plants using overhead monorails. The environment is pleasant, clean, and amazingly quiet. The workers all seem quite professional in their attitudes and are always willing to share information about 'their' AGV system.

GM of Canada Oshawa – rear axle assembly*

In late 1986, the GM-10 world car project will affect the Oshawa Car Final Assembly Plant #2. The present 'H' car build process, incorporating standard dc chain drive conveyance systems, is scheduled to be replaced by electrified monorail systems (EMS) and AGV systems. In an effort to prepare engineering, maintenance and production personnel, a pilot programme was developed.

The initial phase of this programme was to introduce AGVs by implementing a small subassembly system. In January 1986, the rear axle pedestal conveyor was replaced by a 12-vehicle AGV system. This particular application was selected because it

---

* This case study was written by William V. Pratt, Plant Electrical Engineer, Car Final Assembly, GM of Canada Oshawa, Ontario.

demonstrated a number of concepts in production, such as stock kitting, stopped workstations, parallel processing, interfacing with a gantry robot, and production throughput requirements. Additional merits of this application were available turn-around space for project development, no load-tracking requirements since the build process was sequential, and actual assembly on the AGV rather than a simple delivery system.

The basic layout of this system included five manual stations and one robotic workcell as shown in Fig. 13.10. Station 1 is for stock kitting and axle scheduling. Two operators are required to select the appropriate brake lines, track bar, and fastening devices and load them onto the AGV. Station 2 is axle load and scheduling conformation. With the axle and all necessary items for subassembly loaded, the AGV moves into Station 3. At this point, the vehicles separate into two parallel-processing lanes for production assembly. These lanes are a 'first in, first out' configuration designed to maintain production sequence. A total of four operators (two per lane) are used for the subassembly. If the operators experience difficulty in the assembly process, they have the ability to hold the vehicle and conduct the appropriate

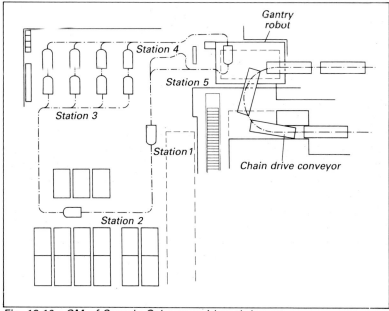

Fig. 13.10 GM of Canada Oshawa guidepath layout

repairs. On leaving Station 3, the vehicles merge back into one lane. Station 4 is for track-bar assembly and inspection re-torque. After this operation, the AGV moves into the robotic workcell for automatic unload. Here the completed axle is transferred to the main line. The AGV system throughput is directly coupled to the main line assembly rate.

The robotic workcell has demonstrated system interface at the discrete I/O level. Precision stopping of the AGV is required for the robot to be able to interface with it. Station 5 is the manual back-up for the robot and is bypassed under normal production operation.

Another major concept demonstrated by this particular system is that it is controlled by a programmable logic controller (PLC). Although several AGV vendors initially specified higher levels of control, Oshawa Car Assembly demanded that its systems operate with a PLC architecture. This was considered necessary to ensure a competent level of understanding and an ease of maintainability from within the maintenance department.

Timing of this project was also considered critical with respect to its functionality. To provide the benefits of being a pilot system, it would have to be installed as soon as possible. This project was contracted in June 1985, and the system was functional by 31 December 1985. With a few months' lead-time before the scheduled beginning of the W car change-over, many of the concepts demonstrated or developed with this small project will be incorporated in the main line system.

In summary:

There is considerable interest in using AGV systems in assembly processes amongst both industrial users and AGV suppliers. Several assembly systems have been installed in the USA during the past two years and much experience has been gained. Future systems should be able to be designed with considerably fewer problems than have been experienced in the past. Also, simulation is improving which will help isolate potential problem areas while the system is still in the design stage. A user should not be afraid to proceed but before doing so should definitely visit as many facilities as possible that use AGV system assembly and learn all they can about the systems.

Chapter Fourteen

AGVs in electronics manufacturing

Over the past decade, nearly all segments of the electronics industry have shown substantial growth; indeed, it has become one of the largest manufacturing industries in the USA. As production costs escalate, many electronics plants are investigating new and innovative methods to counteract this problem. Automation is a prime solution since it can reduce production costs and space requirements, while at the same time increasing productivity and product quality. This trend towards automation has recently increased the importance of AGVs for cost savings and as potential integrators of material handling, and this is rapidly becoming evident to electronics industries. Although AGVs are now appearing in a variety of areas, from wafer fabrication to computer assembly, applications in electronics manufacturing are still relatively few and far between, and those who do have systems are reluctant to share any information for fear of helping their competitors.

The case studies presented in this chapter are therefore general in nature and, in some cases, the user company's name is not given. The only AGV systems that users were willing to discuss are general material-handling and storage applications similar to those presented in Chapter Twelve. Applications where AGVs are integrated into manufacturing processes are definitely restricted.

Special considerations

As is basically true with each general type of application, there are unique considerations for electronics manufacturing. One of the most important considerations is the environment in which the vehicle must operate since many of the electronics manufacturing operations must take place in a clean room where contaminants in the air must be restricted to a few parts per million. This almost eliminates the possibility of using wire-guided vehicles since slotting or cutting the floors to install the guidewire would contaminate the entire clean room. As a result, many electronics manufacturers are using optical guidepath vehicles or one of the new guidance techniques, such as infrared, pattern recognition, or gyros. Surface-mounted copper-conductive guidepaths have also been used successfully.

Another important consideration is the vehicle size and payload capacity. In the past, most vehicles were designed for warehousing or assembly operations with large payloads. Since most products in the electronics industry are small and very light-weight, the vehicle size and payload required is significantly less. The electronics industry requires new designs for light-load AGVs and many suppliers are responding to that demand.

General case study*

In the early days of printed circuit board (pcb) production, the assembly process was highly labour intensive. The obvious problems, such as high labour costs, poor quality, and new board layouts requiring ongoing training programmes, forced manufacturers to automate. The resultant 'islands' of automation, include insertion machines that are preprogrammed (based on board type) to apply certain components to the circuit boards which are then advanced to other stations for further processing. Different board types require different components, and thus different machine sequences.

For situations where there are high volumes and low model mixes of boards, conveyors are effectively used to bridge the stations. However, the trend is away from high volumes of any one circuit board and toward moderate volumes of many different types. This makes the use of conveyors very difficult since the various types of board will be routed differently. A truly flexible or

---

*This case study is a composite of several AGV system installations in various electronics manufacturers of printed circuit boards. It is based on a brochure published by Volvo Automated Systems, a division of Volvo of North America.

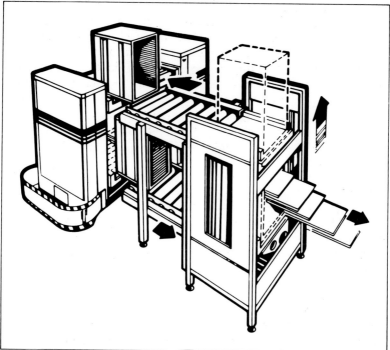

Fig. 14.1 *AGV depositing/picking up magazines of circuit boards*

programmable transporting system is needed – an ideal application for AGVs. Additional benefits obtained from using AGVs include improved machine access and machine deployment.

With the conveyor system, boards were handled individually but with the adoption of AGVs, the boards are transported in magazines. The AGV deposits a full magazine of boards at one end of the pass-through insertion machine and picks up an empty magazine as shown in Fig. 14.1. The boards are removed mechanically by the machine and the insertion process begins. On completion, the boards are transported through to the other side of the machine where they are mechanically loaded into another magazine, picked up by the AGV, and taken to the next operation. Whenever a machine needs another magazine of boards to be delivered or has a full magazine of completed boards to be picked up, the controller issues appropriate orders to the AGVs. Fig. 14.2 shows the Volvo Lifting Rollertable Auto Carrier designed specifically for electronics assembly applications.

Fig. 14.2   The Volvo AGV designed specifically for electronics manufacturing

Various electronics manufacturers using AGVs have achieved a truly flexible material-handling system that:

- Supports moderate- and low-volume production.
- Can be readily integrated with other forms of automation.
- Provides access to machines.
- Is much simpler than complex conveying systems.
- Provides floor-space savings.

Specific case studies

Magnetic Peripherals, Inc. (Twin Cities Disk Division)*

Magnetic Peripherals, Inc., manufactures magnetic disk drives (computer peripheral equipment) for Control Data Corporation. The disk drives must operate within millionths of an inch

---

*This case study is based on an article published in *Modern Materials Handling*, June 1985, entitled 'AGVs boast productivity in assembly', and on a presentation by Dan P. Dooley, Manager of HDA Manufacturing, Magnetic Peripherals, Inc., Bloomington, Minnesota, at AGVS '85 sponsored by the Material Handling Institute.

tolerances, so even the smallest contaminants can cause the drive to malfunction while being used. This necessitates that the head disk assembly be accomplished in a clean-room environment where the air is filtered to control particle size to 0.5μm per 100ft^3 (2.8m^3). (A human being emits approximately 150,000 particles of that size per minute.) A positive pressure also ensures that no contaminants will enter the work area.

Another problem is that during assembly there is only two-thousandths of an inch clearance around the spindle, and any part touching the spindle can create contaminants. Since humans cannot hold such tolerances, it was decided that the assembly was best accomplished by use of several vision-guided robots. It was also deterimed that conveyors consumed too much of the workcell space and, although good at transporting parts, were not good at transferring and precisely locating a workpiece in a workcell. AGVs offered a good alternative, providing transportation, using relatively little space, precision transfer, and flexibility. Measurements at the back wheel of a vehicle have shown that far fewer particles or contaminants are emitted by an AGV than by a person walking around the room. Thus, AGVs can meet the stringent requirements of a clean-room environment.

Fig. 14.3   Magnetic Peripherals' head disk assembly using AGVs

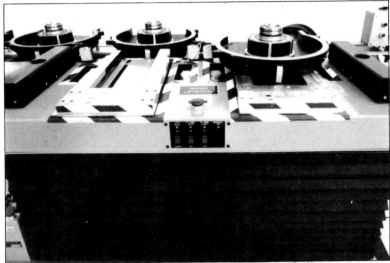

Fig. 14.4   Work platform for transferring head disk assembly

For this application, two optically guided Litton 800 series 'smart carts' were selected to deliver in-process head disk assembly components to four automated workcells (Fig. 14.3). Each vehicle's work platform consists of a lift mechanism and two fork units to shuttle the load to and from the workstation (Fig. 14.4). Communication between the robotic workstation and the vehicles is accomplished by two methods: one is through a computer link with information being downloaded to the vehicle through radio frequency (FM), the other through Omronn infrared sensors at each workstation.

The work platform was engineered by Magnetic Peripherals, while Litton was responsible for the detailed design work and interface to the vehicle. The two shuttle mechanisms allow the AGV to pick up a completed head assembly from a workstation while delivering the next assembly to be worked on. Positioning is accomplished using optical sensors on the vehicles and on the forks.

The guidepath (chemically treated tape) layout is shown in Fig. 14.5. At the first workstation, the bottom half of a disk drive casting is loaded from a conveyor onto the AGV. The vehicle then proceeds to the second workstation where the casting is unloaded and two vision-guided robots perform several assembly operations. One robot stacks disks and three other components on the

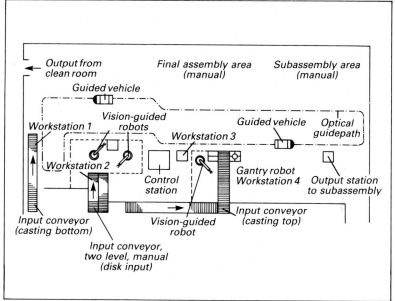

Fig. 14.5 *Magnetic Peripherals' clean room guidepath layout*

spindle of the assembly; a vision system then ensures that the disks are stacked level and determines the orientation of the screw holes. The second robot then drives six screws into the assembly. When the next AGV arrives, the disk assembly is transferred to the vehicle for delivery to the third workstation at which another vision-guided robot drives the six screws to their specified torque. Another AGV then transports the completed head assembly to the next workstation where a gantry robot picks up the top half of a casting from the conveyor, places it over the assembly, and carefully applies the required straight-line force to avoid throwing the aligned bearing off-centre. After the two halves of the casting are seated, the robot applies and drives 12 screws to secure the assembly. Besides the bearing alignment, the vision system also checks for levelness at this point. The AGV then picks up the completed assembly and delivers it to the output station where subsequent assembly operations are performed manually.

The benefits derived from this application have been substantial: damage to the head assembly due to handling has been eliminated, product rejects have greatly decreased while productivity has more than doubled, and at the same time, there has been a two-thirds reduction in the labour force. The vast majority of rejects prior to the introduction of this system were caused by handling damage that disrupted the extremely close tolerances on the disk assemblies.

The flexibility offered by the AGV system, especially its guidepath, has permitted the reduction of space required to produce the head disk assembly. The guidepath was modified to accommodate the improvements made on the equipment used in the production process. The reduction in the space requirements for the build area for the one product has made it possible to add an entirely new product line into the existing work area.

Intel Corporation*

Intel Corporation is committed to be the world-class manufacturer and leader of technology. A highly automated factory in Chandler, Arizona was built to be able to produce and deliver high quality products rapidly and at low prices. This factory employs advanced equipment, including an AGV system for material handling.

The AGV system is used in an integrated circuit assembly facility which consists of the following sequential processes: wafer sawing, die attaching, wire bonding, moulding, trimming and forming, lead soldering, and packing/shipping. The material handling involves moving input material from the inventory area to the manufacturing area and returning output materials back to inventory. At present, the AGV system is limited to servicing the moulding, trimming/forming, lead soldering, and package/shipping processes. If material is requested by a deposit station (locations 1, 4, 6, 9 in Fig. 14.6) in the manufacturing area, the AGV goes to the appropriate inventory pick-up station (11–14), picks up the requested material and then proceeds to deliver it. If the request is to remove material from one of the pick-up stations (2, 3, 5, 7 or 8), the AGV will proceed to pick up the material and then deliver it to the inventory deposit station (10). Table 14.1 lists the types of process associated with each station, as well as the type of material being transferred. All material is carried in trays 24 × 16 × 8in. (approx. 61 × 41 × 20cm) in size.

The AGV is the smart Litton Model 500 and communication is by infrared at selected locations. Upon completing an assignment,

---

*This case study is based on a paper by Shay-Ping T. Wang, Intel Corporation, entitled 'Planning an automatic guided vehicle system using animated graphic simulation'.

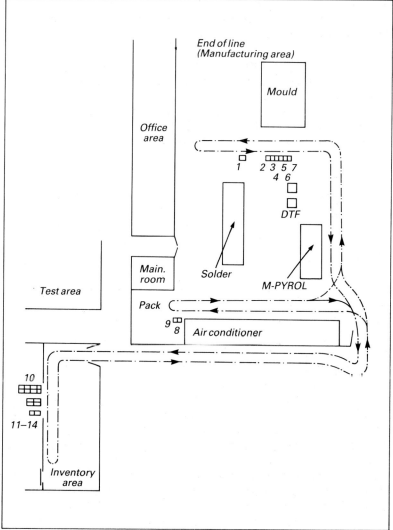

Fig. 14.6 Intel Corporations' IC assembly facility layout

the AGV proceeds to the next communication point for further assignments. If there are no further assignments, the vehicle will proceed to its home position and wait for further instructions.

The work platform is designed to carry two tote trays and contains shuttle mechanisms which can load and unload two totes

Table 14.1 Process and material transferred for each station (Intel Corp.)

Station	Process	Deposit material	Pick up material
1	Soldering	Tube	–
2	Soldering	–	Empty tote
3	Mould A	–	Scrap
4	Mould A	Compound A	–
5	Mould B	–	Scrap
6	Mould B	Compound B	–
7	Trimming/forming	–	Scrap
8	Packing/shipping	–	Finish product
9	Packing/shipping	Empty box	–
10	Inventory input	Output materials*	–
11	Material for Station 4	–	Compound A
12	Material for Station 6	–	Compound B
13	Material for Station 9	–	Empty box
14	Material for Station 1	–	Tube

*Empty totes, scrap and finished product

from two docks simultaneously (Fig. 14.7). Since a request for material transfer involves a single tote, the system capacity would be reduced by 50% if only one tote were handled per trip. To increase the system efficiency, a control delay concept was developed to force as many two-load trips as possible. Upon receiving a request, the central controller will not dispatch the AGV unless either another request occurs or the AGV has waited for a specified time (control delay).

Fig. 14.7 The Litton Model 500 AGV used at Intel

A sensor at each dock detects the presence of a tote and gives the indicated results to the central controller. When an operator removes a tote from a deposit dock or places a tote on a pick-up dock, the sensor is triggered, thus signifying a request. The dispatch of an AGV is based on the priority level associated with that dock. Priority levels are based on the cycle time of a tote at that particular workstation – the shorter the workstation time, the higher the priority of that station. Workstation cycle times range from 22min (priority 1) for station 1, to 80min (priority 9) for station 5.

Printed wire board test facility

A lot of constraints were placed on an industrial engineering team at a printed wire board (pwb) test facility when they tried to maximise the production areas of an existing building. At the same time, they had to maintain the flexibility required and in order to meet the customers' needs, production processes had to be able to be set up to support both older and new products.

The manufacturing engineering department carries out a quarterly work-sampling study for the test department (the largest production department). Through these studies, one of the areas of concern identified was the amount of time taken to transport pwbs within the test areas. These material-handling activities were being accomplished by test technicians and repair operators. The impact on the test department was:

- Approximately 5% of the production time was being lost while direct production employees were away from their work-stations performing material-handling activities.
- Carts being used to transport pwbs occupied a significant amount of test area space.
- Using carts to transport pwbs increased the work-in-progress inventory.

A number of alternative approaches were therefore studied.

Material handlers. Hiring several extra people to accomplish the test department's material-handling activities would have yielded the following results:

- A 5% increase in available production time (+).
- Slightly lower cost than the existing method (+).

- Flexibility to changes in the production flow (+).
- Increased number of carts and space occupied (−).
- Increased work-in-progress inventory (−).

Conveyors. Installing a conveyor system would:

- Provide a 5% increase in available production time (+).
- Provide a low annual operating cost (+).
- Provide a reduction in the work-in-progress inventory (+).
- Require a high initial investment (−).
- Provide no reduction in floor-space used – possibly even an increase (−).
- Provide little flexibility in adapting to production-flow changes (−).

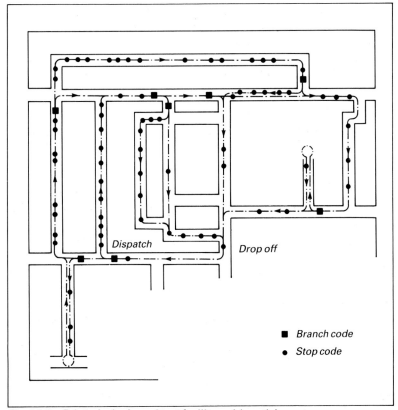

Fig. 14.8   Printed wire board test facility guidepath layout

AGV system. Installing an AGV system provided the following results:

- A 5% increase in available production time (+).
- Low annual operating cost (+).
- Significant reduction in the floor-space required (+).
- Considerable flexibility to changes in the production flow, based on using a chemical guidepath (+).

Based on the evaluation of the available alternatives, the installation of an AGV system best satisfied the decision criteria. In this specific situation, where flexibility was a prime consideration, a Litton Model 400 AGV, which uses a chemical guidepath, was selected. Changes in the 600ft (approx. 180m) guidepath can be made quickly by in-house personnel. Fig. 14.8 shows the guidepath layout with its eight branches and 60 potential stops. The AGV system was installed in August 1985 and, although the actual savings have not been calculated yet, the estimated labour savings alone will reduce the cost of transporting pwbs by 60%. The process will be changed in the future which will considerably increase the throughput and require a second AGV.

Radio and analogue products

A large operation that produces electronic products occupies 250,000ft² (approx. 23,000m²). This size, coupled with the high-volume material-handling requirement, drove the industrial engineering department to identify a means to automate the material transportation. Also, the mail volume was large enough to justify automation. The solution was to install two AGV systems.

The first system, installed in 1983, consisted of two Raymond Electote Model 55 AGVs running in the manufacturing area. Two other suppliers were considered, but the overall rating, including cost, service, quality and flexibility, led to the Raymond equipment being chosen.

It was evident that a constraint with the existing aisle width would restrict the vehicles' path through the main aisles to no less than 8ft (approx. 2.5m). Except between Stations 2 and 13, the vehicles travel only one way which avoids collisions (Fig. 14.9). An additional control is placed on this segment to avoid sending a vehicle to the stock-room if there is already a vehicle on this route. The total length of the route is about 1500ft (approx. 760m) along

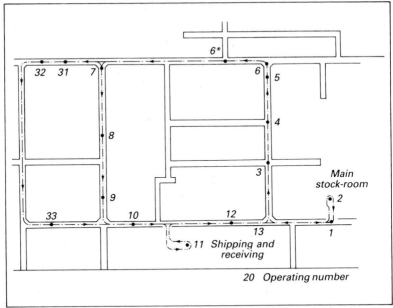

Fig. 14.9   Guidepath layout

the main loop. A second loop is used only when a transaction happens at stations 31, 32 or 33, as shown in the layout.

An important aspect is that the safety bumpers have been modified by adding vertical posts, because in certain cases the bumpers were going under an obstacle without touching it, thus creating an accident risk. Yellow floor-marks show the vehicles' path and help people realise the vehicles' destination, especially at intersections. The vehicles are also equipped with a warning 'beep' and a yellow flashing signal.

A preventive maintenance programme reduces the down-time to an acceptable minimum level. Each vehicle is inspected and lubricated each month. The system's acceptance by all employees prevented any personnel problems. A memorandum was sent to all personnel explaining how the vehicles work and how to use them, as well as all the safety features.

The second AGV system serves the office area. A Bell & Howell Mailmobile Model 9100B delivers mail and small parcels. The vehicle runs along a 28-station circuit at a speed of 107ft/min (approx. 32.5m/min). Safety stops are made at all main intersections.

The two AGV systems share one aisle between Stations 6 and 6*, as shown in Fig. 14.9. To avoid a collision between vehicles, a signal transmitter is installed on each Raymond vehicle and a signal receiver on the Mailmobile. The Raymond Electote AGVs always have the right-of-way – the Mailmobile stops to let the other AGVs go by before continuing on its own journey.

Printed wire board production and test area

This operating module is organised as a self-contained production centre within a large manufacturing organisation. In 1983, the centre was facing a tremendous challenge – the forecast for 1984-86 called for twice the 1983 production figures, along with the day-to-day efforts to reduce costs and improve productivity and quality.

To reduce the cost of material handling, and to improve material flow between workstations, the manufacturing engineering department had considered roller conveyors, belt transporters, overhead chain transporters and AGVs. Although the cheapest solution was the belt transporter and the most flexible one was manual handling, an AGV system was selected.

The requirements for the module's transport system were:

- High flexibility at low cost.
- Small overall size with less than 500lb (approx. 225kg) payload.
- System modularity – growth from one vehicle to two or more.
- Control upgradability – from manual to manual/computer.
- Safety features (an important consideration).

When the Litton vehicles were investigated it was discovered that a vehicle for office use was also manufactured (the Mailmobile marketed by Bell & Howell). With several hundred vehicles delivering mail and small parcels, the safety features had already been proven for the office environment.

However, its cousins, the Litton vehicles, were ruggedised for industrial use and had a greater intelligence capacity. At one end of the product line was a smart '400' Series vehicle. This vehicle was manually programmable and could interpret location and function codes printed on the floor. At the other end of the product line, Litton UHS had the '800' Series (a 'dumb' vehicle driven by a VAX computer) which had the necessary requirements for a sophisticated manufacturing process.

The existence of both the 400 and 800 Series was very important

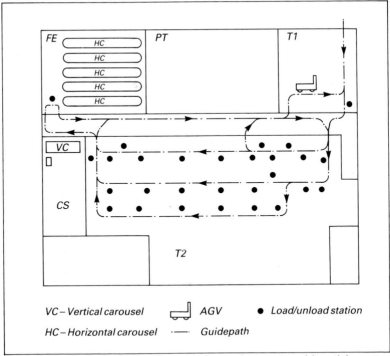

Fig. 14.10   Printed wire board production and test area guidepath layout

for the implementation strategy. This called for starting with one 400 Series vehicle and progressing to more vehicles with more complex controls. The layout shown in Fig. 14.10 consists of approximately 500ft (approx. 150m) of optical guidepath and 40 stations. At the same time, Litton UHS was developing a new vehicle, a hybrid between the 400 and 800, keeping all the intelligent features of the 400 and enhancing it with computer communication capabilities.

The first vehicle was delivered in May 1984 and, from May to October 1985, the vehicle system and personnel went through all sorts of testing, learning, educating, selling and PR activities. At that time, the engineering team was satisfied with the vehicle's performance and safety features, and was in a better position to design the system to make optimum use of the AGV's capabilities. The vehicle also met the safety standards set by management and unions. In November 1985, the vehicle started two-shift operation.

Robotic vehicles in semiconductor processing*

The continued need for automating manufacturing processes in clean-room environments requires transport systems to provide material movement between process equipment. In addressing the requirements for automated clean-room manufacturing, flexibility and cleanliness of transport equipment are predominant. Flexible Manufacturing Systems, Inc., has developed a robotic vehicle with an inertial guidance system and with a better than Class 10 particulate generation feature. The vehicle system has been operating in a semiconductor production facility in an automated wafer-handling system.

Initially, the robotic vehicle (Fig. 14.11) is taught its path and transfer movements through a teach pendant. Path movements are determined through the inertial guidance system, providing directional data, and an optical encoder coupled to the drive wheel measures distance travelled. The beginning and end of each path (the docking locations for material transfer) are the 'learning points'. A mirror mounted 38in. (approx. 96.5mm) off the floor surface is scanned upon docking, and by interpreting the reflections the vehicle triangulates its position. The vehicle's coordinates, distance from the mirror, and its angular orientation, are then provided to the arm and navigational computers. The arm computer compensates arm movement to achieve the position originally taught, while the navigation system compensates for directional and distance error accumulated during prior movement.

The vehicle utilises a six-axis robotic arm for loading/unloading vehicles docked at intelligent work-in-process (WIP) stations and process equipment. With the patented optical docking system, equipment is not touched, thus eliminating vibration. The six-axis arm provides the dexterity to load containers into the precise location (typically within ±0.015in. (0.4mm)). Cleanliness is achieved through the use of special materials and drawing air through the vehicle body. With such a vehicle initially working amongst personnel, safety systems were incorporated. Sonar around the vehicle indicates obstacle detection, a voice module instructs the obstacle to move, and touch sensitive outer panels stop the vehicle if contact is made.

---

*This case study was written by G. (John) Foggiato, Director – Technical Marketing, Flexible Manufacturing Systems, Inc., Los Gatos, California.

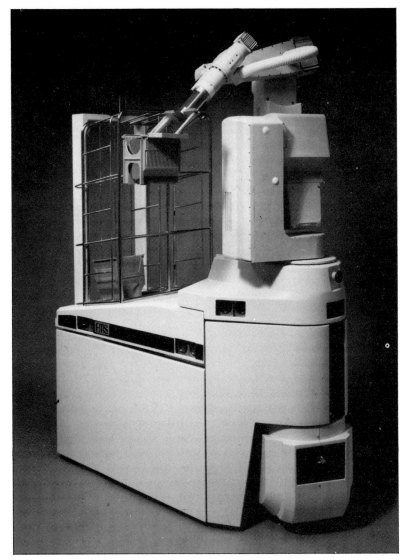

Fig. 14.11   The robotic vehicle

Typical applications involve movement of materials between
WIP stations and process equipment. An actual installation in a
clean-room environment showing the guidepath is illustrated in
Fig. 14.12. The vehicle must also pass through two doors,

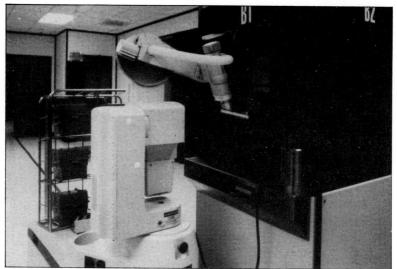

Fig. 14.12   View of installation

activated by computer control. With the infrared communication system, the vehicle continuously relays its location and status to the system computer, which then activates the door-opening mechanism allowing the vehicle to pass. With real-time location information provided, a graphical display of vehicle movement is provided at the system's supervisory control terminal. This gives an instant picture of where vehicles are moving, which stations are being serviced, and any priorities being addressed.

Infrared communication via an omnidirectional transceiver continually provides data to indicate vehicle status, schedule new movements, change vehicle routes and monitor material lot identification. Routes are developed as a series of paths. As material lots are entered into the system, their process flow in the form of routes is also entered. Transport then follows the designated routing. If restrictive time limits are placed on transfers, lots become prioritised.

Although the system layout shows a path loop (Fig. 14.13), the vehicle does move backwards and forwards. This provides path movement optimisation and allows priorities to be addressed. Upon loading/unloading a process station, the vehicle evaluates how to reach the next destination, and may move forward or reverse as needed.

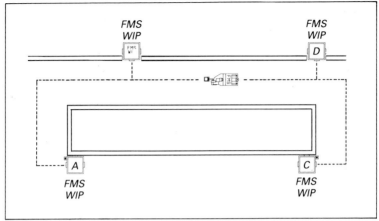

Fig. 14.13   Automated wafer handling system layout

As the vehicle is battery powered, a unique battery recharging method is utilised. In clean-room applications, battery change-out is not desired due to vehicle exposure to contamination. The vehicle employs a magnetic coupled opportunity charging system. Upon docking at a station with the recharging module, the vehicle arm initially plugs in, allowing recharge during arm movements. When finished, it unplugs and the vehicle moves on.

The vehicle is 22in. wide (approx. 56cm), 48in. long (approx. 122cm) and stands 60in. high (approx. 152cm). The total weight is 600lb (approx. 270kg), the principal weight element being the batteries. The front drive-wheel housing incorporates the inertial guidance system coupled to the optical encoder. If the vehicle needs to turn around, the front wheel turns more than 90° to minimise the turning radius. At the rear of the vehicle, a cargo bay provides in-transit storage of containers.

In summary:

With the electronics manufacturing industry being so competitve, all possible methods to reduce production costs, work-in-progress, and space requirements are being sought. At the same time, increases in productivity and product quality are required. It is evident that a flexible material-handling system is needed to meet these requirements. Many electronics manufacturers are turning to AGVs to meet their needs and with considerable success. However, because of the competitive nature of this business, companies are generally reluctant to share information about the benefits of AGV systems. As a result, systems are usually only discussed in general terms, without reference to the product, process, or even the company name.

Chapter Fifteen

AGVs in FMS

As exhibited by the number of books, technical papers, and conferences on the subject, FMS is an area of considerable interest. Manufacturing industries are encountering requirements of their facilities never experienced before. For example, it is now required that they react quickly to changing markets, to increasing numbers of product variations, and to short product life-cycles. These factors all require that modern manufacturing facilities have a high degree of flexibility, the ability to manufacture a range of similar products on the same equipment, and the ability to change tooling quickly so as to manufacture new variations of the products in response to market demand. Thus, the goal is to be able to accommodate short lead-times while at the same time incurring minimum tooling costs. Today, it is necessary to obtain the same efficiencies for low- and medium-batch production as is experienced in mass-volume systems.

An obvious solution to this is to use a number of manufacturing and assembly cells capable of covering the range of tasks required to satisfy production of the various product families. While the initial expense for such a flexible manufacturing system is high, changes require minimal further investments. Well-designed manufacturing cells will operate independently without constraints imposed by other cells or equipment. As such, various families of parts will require multiple flow-paths through the cells and will be even more complex when handling multiple families.

To handle such complex material-handling problems, the key link in FMS is to use an AGV system operating at a high level of intelligence. A major consideration is that an AGV system be under full computer control and have the ability to integrate into the facility's host management computer. It can make a significant contribution to the total flow of data required for production and inventory control. Other advantages of an AGV system used in an FMS application are as follows:

- Optimises the efficiency of the handling system.
- Reduction of labour force (especially clerks).
- Operation of unmanned shifts.
- Better utilisation of expensive equipment.
- More freedom than is offered by other types of handling devices.
- Handles complex production rates as well as product routing.
- Extension of the number of operating stations permissible.
- Allows a variety of vehicles to perform different functions on the same system.
- Can work with either parallel or series arranged machine groups.

Special considerations

The AGV system will only be able to meet the requirements of a flexible manufacturing system if it is properly designed. The AGV system needs to be designed to accommodate the different types of vehicles required to meet the needs. Items that need to be transported and considered during design of the AGV system include:

- Raw materials.
- Manufactured parts between cells.
- Completed parts to assembly.
- Preset perishable tooling.
- Fixturing.
- Purchased parts to assembly cells.
- Maintenance material.
- Chips and swarf.

To meet these requirements, several types of vehicles (e.g. unit load carriers and pallet trucks), must be considered, taking into account the size and load capacity required. Fig. 15.1 illustrates an AGV in an FMS application. The AGV system will also need to be designed so that the vehicles will be able to move freely from any

Fig. 15.1   AGV in an FMS application

point to a possible required sequential point. The guidepath and control system should also be designed to accommodate future expansion or rearrangement.

The AGV must interface with many types of CNC machines, robots, AS/RS, conveyors, and assembly workstations in an FMS. There must be some method provided for precision docking, such as by the use of cones, and some type of interlock security. It is necessary to verify that the right parts have been delivered (since a pallet of wrong parts could do considerable damage to the machines and tooling). Pallet orientation and the fact that it is seated in its fixturing should also be verified. The station receiving the parts should check its own status (e.g. correct tooling, ready for parts, etc.) and verify the correct criteria.

A possible method of processing small batches of material is to use family-of-parts tray concepts. Trays can be designed to handle a range of part families. These trays will maintain orientation of the parts during handling, minimise part damage, allow for robot interfacing, and can provide controlled buffer sizes between operations. The trays can be permanently coded so that their family and the exact part can be identified. For some situations, machine-tool pallets complete with fixturing and components may be used.

In addition, the coolants, chips, oil and swarf associated with machining operations must be kept off the floor and prevented from interfering with the operation of other equipment such as the AGVs or AS/RS. A drip-tray should therefore be designed and built in such a manner that any of these foreign materials will be contained until they can be properly disposed of. All machine parts should be washed or cleaned before being returned to storage or delivered to the assembly area.

Many FMS installations are tied to a high density storage AS/RS, but this is not consistent with 'just-in-time' concepts. Other FMS installations are beginning to use mini AS/RS that support just-in-time, by providing staging of small amounts of incoming raw material and by accommodating small variable buffers for work-in-progress materials. The AGV system can be tied into the AS/RS to provide complete material inventory and control. The objective is to reverse the practice of 95% waiting time and 5% manufacturing time – a well thought out and designed material-handling system can be integrated into an FMS to provide that reality.

Case studies

LTV Aerospace and Defense Company – Vought Aero Products Division*

The LTV Aerospace and Defense Company's Vought Aero Products Division has one FMS in production and another which is currently being designed and developed. The FMC I is the result of an evolutionary implementation of a multiproduct factory of the future. The project called for machining more than 500 different parts for the B-1B fuselage and was done in conjunction with the US Department of Defense, the US Air Force, and Rockwell International for the B-1B technology modernisation project.

The flexibility offered by FMS is especially applicable to the relatively small lot sizes typical of the aerospace industry. A well-designed FMS can produce small lot sizes economically and can ease the transition from one product to the next. The flexible machining cell (FMC) has demonstrated a three-fold productivity

---

* This case study is based on a paper by J.S. Leitch, Facilities Systems Project Manager, entitled 'Flexible machining cell', and on a paper by A.J. Roch, Jr., Director – Industrial Modernisation, entitled 'Productivity by design – FMS applications that work'. Both are employees of Vought Aero Products Division.

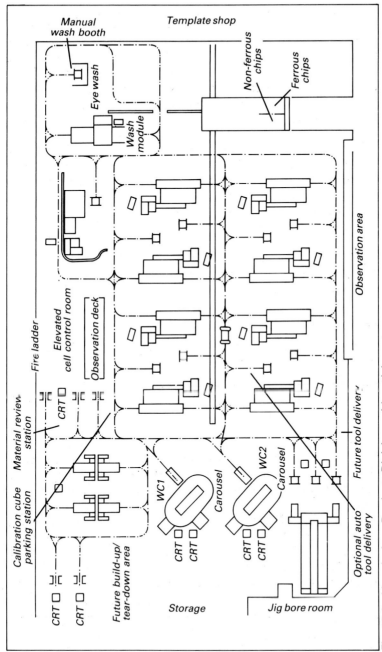

Fig. 15.2 Vought Aero Products Division guidepath layout

improvement over conventional machining and has afforded these productivity gains by reducing human intervention, improving the material handling, improving machine utilisation, enhancing throughput, and maximising operational control.

The FMC consists of eight horizontal single-spindle machining centres (fixtures, tooling, and cutters), two automatic coordinate measuring machines, an automatic wash-station, and four Eaton-Kenway AGVs which transport B-1B parts on machining pallets and have been configured for future integration of an automatic cutter delivery system to transport tool magazines within this cell. Fig. 15.2 shows the guidepath layout.

An average part passes through the FMC three times: the first pass involves milling one side of the part blank for tooling holes, the second produces the first features of the part, and the third pass completes the part. The part production starts with an operator loading blanks `onto pallets which are then moved automatically onto one of two carousels that hold up to ten pallets

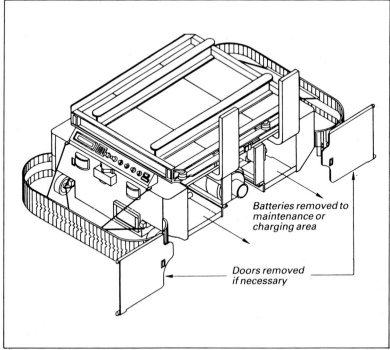

Batteries removed to
maintenance or
charging area

Doors removed
if necessary

Fig. 15.3   Robocarrier lifting detail

each. They remain on the rotating carousels until the cell is ready to machine the part included on a designated pallet. When a pallet is required by the cell, an AGV is dispatched to retrieve it from the carousel and deliver it to the machining centre. Each centre has a total queue capacity of five pallets – two completed and waiting to be transported, one in-process, and two waiting to have their parts machined. The completed parts are transported by the AGVs to the automatic wash-station where chips are removed. An AGV then picks up the pallet with its parts and transports it to the inspection station where the coordinate measuring machine automatically verifies the part geometry. The pallets with their completed parts are then returned to the carousel and forwarded to a load/unload station.

The FMC's control computer receives a 20-day 'window' of work orders on a daily basis from the business host computer. When the FMC computer receives the downloaded data, it automatically accesses the workload to maximise the machining centre resource utilisation. This optimisation is based on consideration of:

- Schedule.
- Priority.
- Material availability.
- NC and inspection part-program availability.
- Cutting tool requirements.
- Fixtures and pallets.
- Machining time.

Based on this, the FMC computer selects enough work orders for a 24-hour production run and then analyses and simulates the work-load to obtain an operation schedule. This schedule is designed to minimise cutter-tool changes, maximise machine utilisation, and reserve a selection of parts with long machining times for the unmanned third shift.

The four Model XK Eaton-Kenway Robocarriers have a maximum work envelope of $36 \times 36 \times 32$in. (approx. $91 \times 91 \times 81$cm) on the square pallet, a maximum load of 5000lb (approx. 225kg), and a 4in. (approx. 10cm) lift/lower height (Fig. 15.3). The vehicles are bidirectional; however, the pick-up and deposit stands and the main guidepaths were designed for one-way travel to maximise throughput. The basic AGV design included the addition of chip/coolant guards at the top of the vehicles to prevent machining coolant from contaminating the AGV's electronics.

Volvo Components Corporation – Engine Division*

The Engine Division of Volvo Components Corporation produces more than 300,000 gasoline engines and 60,000 diesel engines a year. The diesel engine portion of the operation produces seven different sizes of engines, ranging in size from 3 to 12 litre displacement, and are made for use in trucks, buses, marine and industrial applications. To meet Volvo's goal to be a leader in quality, flexibility, productivity, and delivery reliability, several FMSs have been installed and are now operational.

Several criteria were used when establishing the FMSs, including improving capital turnover through high machine utilisation and providing short lead-times to meet customers' demands. The system-design criteria included system flexibility in responding to total volumes, in variations or types, in product-design changes, and introduction of new products.

The first FMS was installed for rough machining of heavy crankshafts and consists of seven different machine groups each with two machines and an automatic gantry loader. The gantries, each equipped with two separate grippers, load and unload the machines with the parts brought in on pallets. There are always two pallets to act as buffer stock between the machines. The crankshafts are transported between the machine groups by two ACS (Volvo) AGVs. The main overall computer controls the machine loaders and AGVs to form an integrated system (Fig. 15.4).

Another system is an FMS for machining heavy timing gear casings and covers. The system consists of two machine groups each of which has a robot for loading/unloading purposes. One of the two groups has a robot travelling on rails servicing three machines. Again, AGVs are used to transport the parts.

The third FMS is for machining exhaust manifolds. Two fork-lift type AGVs transport both fixtures and castings to and from loading stations and also transport the finished products. The pallet fixtures are manually loaded and unloaded with castings, and a loaded fixture is then transported to the first free machine or placed in waiting on the pallet stand. Machine programs are

---

* This case study is based on a paper by R. Murby entitled 'FMS an automation in a diesel engine plant', and on a paper by G. Nordsten entitled 'The evolution of FMS at Volvo Components Corporation in Skovde'. Both are employees of Volvo Components Corporation, Sweden and presented their papers at the 4th International Conference on Flexible Manufacturing Systems.

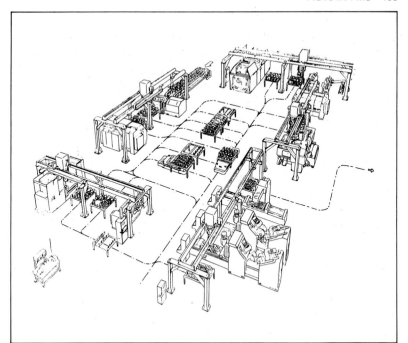

Fig. 15.4   FMS for rough machining of crankshafts

changed automatically during the loading operation. Thirty different manifolds are machined in the system, production being guided by the immediate need in the engine assembly lines (Fig. 15.5). Two highly skilled workers per shift operate this system and also load and unload the pallet fixtures.

Five different types of flywheel for gasoline engines are now being produced by an FMS. The system is similar to the crankshaft FMS – separate machining cells with machine tools loaded by gantry loaders and connected together by AGVs. The design also called for a centre buffer where parts could be stored in case of machine-tool breakage. Because AGVs were used for transportation of pallets, the machines could not be placed in operational sequence but were placed with regard to the handling of chips and the machine size. Forty pallets are used for transporting the flywheels within the system and each pallet can be loaded with 42 flywheels (seven stacks with six on each stack). This leaves one stack position free. Two AGVs are used to transport the pallets of parts between the different machine groups.

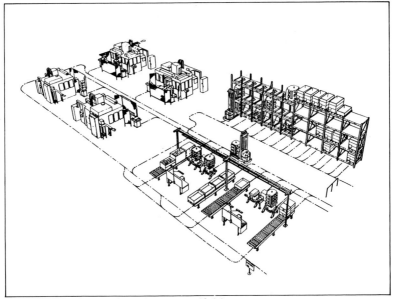

Fig. 15.5   FMS plant for exhaust manifolds

The results of these FMSs, as experienced by Volvo, are:

- In-process time drastically decreased.
- Number of operators decreased by up to 50%.
- Cost reduction per produced component up to 25%.
- Number of machines reduced from 10 to 50%.
- Tool costs 10–20% lower.
- Investment cost increased more than 20%.
- Operator skill requirements increased substantially.

Other benefits that have also appeared are higher quality, fewer rejects, reduction of inspection costs, better ergonomics, and lower noise levels.

In summary:

Although true FMS applications are still few in number, considerable interest is being given to FMS, with large companies establishing pilot systems. To meet customer product demands with short lead-times and minimal tooling costs, it is necessary to consider FMSs and to obtain the required degree of material-handling flexibility. Thus an AGV system operating at a high level of intelligence is needed. As with AGVs used in other applications, there are some special considerations in the design and use of AGVs for FMS applications. Vehicles will most likely be used for more than just transporting parts, and thus will also require design features to permit the carrying of fixtures, tooling, waste material, etc. Another major consideration is protecting the vehicle and floor from coolants, oil, and chips associated with machining operations.

Chapter Sixteen

AGVs in non-manufacturing applications

While AGV systems have been taking root in US manufacturing industries, they have also been making an impact in offices and in other non-manufacturing businesses. Applications range from carrying food, laundry, and other supplies in hospitals, to carrying mail, messages, and packages in offices. There are even automatic people carriers.

Special considerations

Each application requires its own unique type of vehicle, guidance technique, and interfacing criteria, creating its own set of special considerations. Since there is such a wide variety of applications that fall into the non-manufacturing area, it is not feasible to list all the possible considerations associated with these uses. It is therefore intended to give only a general impression of the special considerations experienced by this type of vehicle application.

When used in environments such as hospitals and offices, the vehicles will usually be encountering more people, both directly and indirectly, than would be experienced in manufacturing facilities. A vehicle may be required to negotiate a narrow aisle or a blind intersection filled with people who may be unfamiliar with AGVs. The vehicle must therefore contain enough safety features to protect even children, if they should be encountered. Most people in offices and hospitals are less knowledgeable about mechanical and electronic technology than those in manufacturing environments. The vehicles should therefore be user-friendly.

Most hospital and office AGV systems operate on a passive

guidepath. If the guidepath is optical, it requires more maintenance than other types of systems and to increase guidepath life, it may also require special cleaners and cleaning methods different from those used in the past. Another consideration is that trained service personnel and special equipment may be required to replace the guidepath – an added expense. Metal-tape systems, however, require minimal maintenance. It is wise to check with the AGV supplier to verify that a facility's floor covering is compatible with the guidance technique being considered. For example, certain types of carpet may create problems.

In addition, an interface with the doors and elevators will probably be required so that they will work automatically for the vehicle. It is also necessary that the elevator is of sufficient size to accommodate the vehicle if it must travel between floors. Some facilities incorporate a special elevator that services only the AGV.

Finally, some applications will require special vehicle features and system considerations. Some hospitals use AGVs to transport food, laundry, pharmaceutical supplies, laboratory samples, etc. To be thoroughly sanitised, the vehicles require cleaning between each run or task. Also, the vehicles must be designed to exchange their work platforms quickly since each task requires varying capabilities – delivering food has different storage requirements from carrying laboratory samples or reports.

Case studies

University of Michigan replacement hospital programme

The University of Michigan replacement hospital programme in Ann Arbor, Michigan has undertaken a project to replace or renovate the physical structures that make up the University of Michigan hospital complex. As a result of many years of study and planning, the hospital has been designed to be both attractive and functional well into the next century. With the intention of incorporating the latest in hospital material management systems, the programme called for the use of an AGV system for distributing bulk supplies through the hospital.

The plan called for a series of hand-pushed carts, each designed for a certain function, such as food or laundry transportation. The carts were specially designed to rest on the lift/lower bed of the AGV while being transported (Fig. 16.1) at the destination point, the vehicle simply lowers its bed and leaves the cart. The system

Fig. 16.1 Cart being transported by vehicle at University of Michigan Hospital

contains a total of 15 Eaton/Kenway Robocarriers and is designed to operate with 13 in service. The vehicle guidance system uses a wire guidepath and rf communication.

The new University Hospital is designed with vertical distribution of functions. The lower four floors (B2, B1, 1 and 2) are devoted to non-medical activities and to diagnostic and treatment functions. The fifth level (Floor 3) contains the mechanical equipment, and the upper six floors (4-9) house in-patient units (Fig. 16.2). Floor B2 houses the non-medical activities such as the food preparation, medical and pharmaceutical supplies (Fig. 16.3). Dietetics services prepare the food, cool it for delivery, and send it by AGV to the proper patient-care areas where it is later reheated. Likewise, by use of AGVs, the central material management sends medical supplies and linen, and the pharmacy prepares and sends pharmaceutical supplies to the appropriate areas.

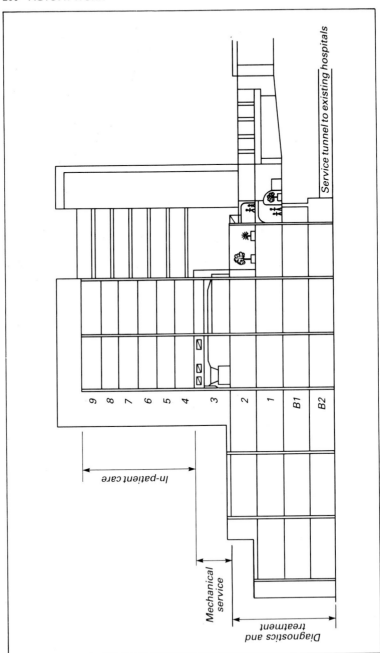

Fig. 16.2   Vertical section of the new University of Michigan Hospital

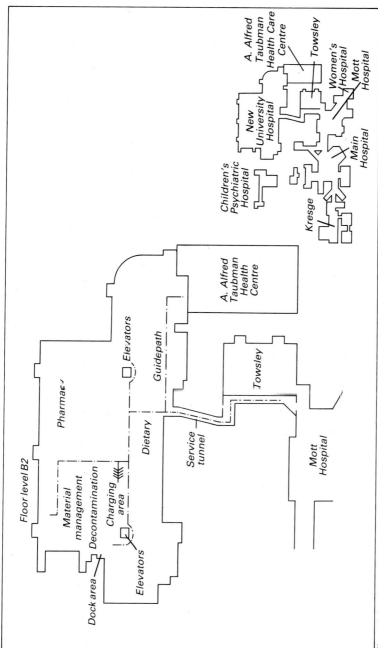

Fig. 16.3 New University Hospital floor layout of level B2 and guidepath layout

Six special material management elevators carry the AGVs and the carts they are transporting to the in-patient floors. Tunnels permit the AGV system to access the other facilities in the complex. The carts return all trash and used supplies to Floor B2, eliminating the need for employees to move the trash from the various floors. The AGV elevators are called by the AGV control system and the vehicles are automatically loaded. The vehicles only travel horizontally on Floor B2, in the holding rooms on the other floors, and in the other hospitals in the complex. On each of the other floors, the AGVs simply deposit the carts in the holding rooms. From these holding rooms, the carts are delivered manually to areas of need. Each in-patient floor also has a satellite pharmacy adjoining the cart-holding area for convenience and safety. These pharmacies are responsible for preparing the unit dose medication.

All vehicles are given their instructions through the main controller, located on Floor B2, which receives requests from the various holding areas through keyboard entry. Also on Floor B2, each trash and soiled cart and vehicle travels to a cart washing-room to be thoroughly sanitised.

Community Hospital laboratory specimen carrier

A new laboratory building was added to Community Hospital in Indianapolis, Indiana. Laboratory samples therefore had to be carried every 30min from the outpatient laboratory in the old building to the central laboratory in the new building, about 500ft (approx. 150m) away. It was decided that an AGV system would provide the most suitable solution to this problem.

The selection was a Litton Series 200 AGV to deliver laboratory samples, reports, and mail between the laboratories. The Series 200 is a flat-bed unit load carrier, so Community Hospital purchased a special cabinet that met their needs and placed this on top of the carrier. Since the guidance is optical, the guidepath consists of a strip of fluorescent material applied directly to the tile floor between the laboratories, and to the carpet in the central laboratory. Personnel at Community Hospital used protective wax to preserve the guidepath and reported no maintenance problems. The vehicle has been in operation for four years, and the hospital is very satisfied with its performance. There have not been any serious problems or accidents during this period. The vehicle travels at 110ft/min (approx. 33.5m/min) and emits a warning beep during automatic travel to alert anyone who is in the pathway.

Leopoldina Hospital's Transcar System*

The Leopoldina Hospital in the city of Schweinfurt, West Germany has been in operation since July 1981. The institution is 'C' shaped with a wing at either end of the main floor system. It has 12 floors with nursing units containing 656 beds on Floors 5–11, diagnostic and treatment centres on Floors 3 and 4, and the remaining floors are dedicated to internal hospital services and support.

Bulk items are automatically transported within the institution by a Transcar AGV system. Over 85,000lb (approx. 38,250kg) of material per day is moved. The system is central processor-controlled and allows for the supply and return of goods to the pharmacy, laboratory, kitchen/dish washing centre, laundry/sterilisation, central supply and the incinerator. The system contains over 210 trolleys (food carts, supply carts, etc.) which are towed by 13 battery-powered guided vehicles (Fig. 16.4). The items moved by the system are pharmaceuticals, laboratory samples, sterile supplies, clean linen, soiled linen, contaminated

Fig. 16.4   Leopoldina Hospital's Transcar vehicle

---

*This case study was written by Robert J. McLendon, Market Manager, TransLogic Corporation.

material, refuse, miscellaneous supplies, as well as three meal deliveries per day. The system transports meals on trays and completes the distribution of 650 meals in less than an hour.

Two elevators in each of the hospital's two wings are used for all vertical transport; two elevators per wing were required to enable the separation of clean and soiled loads. The AGVs do not normally travel on the elevators but are capable of doing so. The total number of vehicles needed to meet system requirements was reduced by enabling the trolleys to travel on elevators without vehicles. A fifth elevator supplies trolleys from the basement storage level to the kitchen.

Trolleys are picked up and delivered to friction roller conveyors located at the entrance to each elevator. These move the trolleys onto the elevator when it is available for loading. When the floor destination has been reached, the trolley is automatically ejected from the elevator by a friction roller conveyor installed in the elevator cabin. Multiple trolleys may queue at certain stations where multiple conveyors are installed in a line. The queue will automatically move up when the first trolley in line is loaded onto the elevator, and conveyors are located at receiving and dispatch stations on each floor to load or empty the elevator. The trolleys are moved manually from the nursing centre to point of use, and, in many cases, are used as the floor storage device.

Horizontal movement of trolleys is performed automatically on two levels. Transcar vehicles shuttle trolleys to the laundry, central supply and trolley storage areas. Also, vehicles deliver trolleys filled with refuse to the incinerator area and drop off trolleys at the entrance to the washing tunnel and pick them up at the washing tunnel exit. The washing tunnel interface is automatic and is without human intervention. When the vehicles are not shuttling trolleys, they are sent to a charging area where they take advantage of opportunity charging.

The AGV system has led to a reduction in man-hours because of its ability to transport the trolleys automatically, load and unload the trolleys, interface with the elevators and take routing instructions from the central processor. It has contributed to a reduction in inventory levels by permitting distribution from central stores on a scheduled or unscheduled basis while reducing pilferage and breakage. Also, the system has given distribution process control to management and has allowed professionals to remain at their work centres leading to improved quality of patient care.

Zale Corporation's Transcar System*

Zale Corporation, the world's largest retailer of fine jewellery, was founded in 1924 by Morris and William Zale of Wichita Falls, Texas. Zale has evolved from that single store operation to a multi-million dollar a year organisation with over 1400 stores worldwide.

In 1980, Zale management announced that corporate headquarters would be transferred from the existing 18-storey Dallas facility to a new six-storey facility to be built in Irving, Texas. At that time all department managers were asked to present their recommendations for personnel, capital equipment and space allocations necessary to ensure the most efficient operations in the new facility. The mail distribution organisation was asked to recommend the most cost-effective and efficient material-handling system which would meet anticipated volume and distribution requirements and, at the same time, be expandable to meet growing demands. The material-handling system had to consolidate the labour intensive functions such as: incoming, outgoing and internal mail processing; pick-up and delivery of packaged freight and accountable materials; distribution of computer reports, office supplies, word processing and copy centre materials; automation of pick-up and delivery of all items required to keep the modern office on the move; and moving accountable materials in a secured environment.

Distribution was to be made to three of the six floors, each floor containing 105,000ft^2 (approx. 32,000m^2) of office space. The automated system had to be capable of interfacing automatically with elevators, service over 1300 employees and handle 14 million pieces of mail per year. Service standards were set to allow pick-up and delivery at 35 stations of mail, copy centre and word processing materials four times daily, accountable materials and computer reports three times daily, and packages, supplies and paper recycling pick-up twice daily. In addition to scheduled deliveries, the capability of sending a vehicle to an individual station without traversing a total floor loop was required to handle station overload conditions. Additional system requirements included: vehicle bidirectional travel which would eliminate the need for double-door elevators and reduce system floor-space requirements, by eliminating the requirement for cul-de-sacs to

---

*This paper is based on a presentation by John Miley, Jr., Manager – Mail Services, Zale Corporation, Irving, Texas.

turn the vehicle around; ease of expansion and economical route relocation; interchangeable trolleys which allowed Zale to design containers to accomplish distribution goals; central processor control which allowed management to control and monitor the distribution process and alter it at will; and finally a system was required which would be compatible with and would enhance the new corporate headquarters' modern office environment.

Zale hired an outside consulting firm to analyse material-handling requirements and to recommend various options from total manual operation to full automation; also included would be an approximate cost including a ten-year cost projection with life-cycle operating costs. After an internal study of the recommendations a product review was made, from which it was apparent that the Transcar system was the most cost-effective and productive system for Zale's requirements.

Transcar was chosen for the following reasons:

- System requirements could be met with five Transcar vehicles and 11 trolleys (Fig. 16.5).
- The payback period was projected as being 2.8 years, but in the event was 2.1 years.

Fig. 16.5   Zale Corporation's Transcar mail vehicle

- Custom design of trolley superstructures allowed Zale to design trolleys best equipped to meet the corporate needs. Trolleys were designed to distribute internal and external mail, to pick up and deliver accountable items (secured trolleys with lock boxes) and computer paper, and to accommodate different size bulk packages (trolleys with movable dividers).
- Central processor control allows control of all distribution activities from a central control area and gives supervisory control to management.
- Trolleys can be sent to a given floor loop and stop at each station for a specified period of time which can be decreased or increased at the station by the operator as required. Also, when required, trolleys can be sent to a specific location without stopping at all stations.
- Personnel requirements were minimised because the system could interface with elevators, single and double doors and the vehicles could charge themselves automatically without human intervention.
- System expansion, relative to the guidance system, is easily attained; the metal tape itself was installed under the floor and was maintenance free.
- The vehicles' multiple-speed capability enhanced the safety aspect of the system.
- The vehicles' bidirectional capability allowed delivery to inaccessible areas without the allocation of floor-space to allow vehicles to turn round.

Transcar has been a cost-effective move for Zale which has drastically improved the service standards and accomplished the goals of an efficient automated material-handling system. Of special note is the fact that Zale currently collects and sells used computer paper, and the revenue generated by this covers Zale's monthly Transcar system maintenance cost.

Signode Corporation's Mailmobile*

When the Signode Corporation moved into its new 'Adcom' building in 1979, it was decided to install an AGV system to deliver its mail. Taking into account the vehicle, the installation costs and a service contract, a short payback period of less than

---

*This case study is based on literature supplied by the Automated Systems Division of Bell & Howell Co.

one year was predicted. A more frequent and regular mail service was also provided – with human messengers, mail would have been picked up and delivered twice a day, while the AGV system offered the same service twice per hour and did not require breaks or days off.

The system services two floors with 859ft (approx. 262m) of guidepath and ten stops at various workstations and offices on the second floor. The third floor has 1130ft (approx. 344m) of guidepath and 21 stops. The vehicles have been programmed to stop at each station for 20s, making the total tour time 20min for the second floor and 30min for the third floor. If 20s is not sufficient, the employee can activate a time-delay switch to hold the machine at a location for a few extra seconds.

The vehicles (Fig. 16.6) contain separate mail trays for each of the workstations or offices at which they stop. To send a message or other material it is necessary simply to place it into the appropriate tray for subsequent pick-up by a colleague. This eliminates the need for employees to leave their desks to deliver mail to their colleagues – an additional cost-saving benefit. Other

Fig. 16.6 Typical Mailmobile

trays are provided for mail that is intended to leave the building, a tray for each of the other divisions and one for external mail. This system allows internal mail to bypass the central mailroom, thus cutting the mailroom's workload by 60%. Mail to other Signode locations and external mail is still handled by the mailroom.

Mailroom clerks are responsible for transferring mail from the mailroom to the vehicles and between the vehicles on the second and third floors. Five minutes before the vehicles reach the elevator area, the mailroom clerks are automatically signalled so that they can meet the vehicles at the elevators. They remove the outgoing mail for another floor or for an external location and add mail to be delivered on that floor.

The Adcom building was planned around open-plan office modules which can be altered to accommodate demands. The optical guidepath allows for quick re-routing if an office complex is internally restricted; the guidepath has also been re-routed to suit the employees' needs.

Westinghouse Furniture System Headquarters

Located in Grand Rapids, Michigan, this is an unique office and manufacturing facility with a most unusual AGV system. The exceptional architecture of the building has been designed in harmony with the function of the furniture, setting it apart from other office/manufacturing facilities. The entire facility has been designed to make technology and productivity easy to achieve. It abounds in the unexpected to promote creativity and thus increase productivity.

Westinghouse Furniture System is a leading manufacturer and marketer of office systems furniture in the USA. To help increase its share of the market, the company built a futuristic office and manufacturing facility instead of a more traditional building and showroom. The office workstations were designed specifically for the task to be done and with each area housing the tools to do that task most efficiently. In essence, the offices are a 'living laboratory' at work. Instead of customers viewing the products in a showroom, they are taken to the various offices to see the products in actual use.

During the conception of the building, it was decided to use an AGV specifically designed to carry customers through the various office and factory areas. Since the doorways are of unusual design, the vehicle was designed to conform to their shape. Fig. 16.7

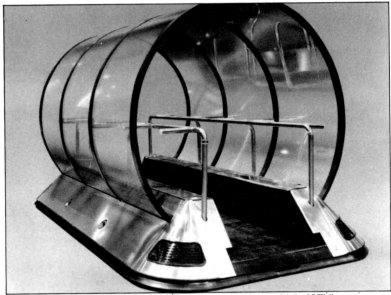

Fig. 16.7   Westinghouse customer transportation vehicle (CTV)

shows the vehicle designed and built by Conco-Tellus. The CTV (Customer Transportation Vehicle) is housed next to the Customer Presentation Centre and is programmed to take customers through several offices, a product test facility, through the manufacturing plant, more offices, past the computer centres, and finally to return to its docking area. Fig. 16.8 shows the guidepath.

The vehicle has been programmed to stop at selected locations where the tour-guide explains the features of that particular area. When the presentation for that station is complete, the guide signals the vehicle to continue to the next stop. In the manufacturing area, there are several visual units at which the vehicle stops and signals the video tape to begin. The video explains the manufacturing processes taking place in the surrounding area. Customers are even encouraged to leave the vehicle to talk to any of the workers in the area and to inspect the quality of their workmanship. A sound-level meter aboard the vehicle measures the surrounding noise level and automatically adjusts the volume of the PA system within the CTV. The tours last between 45min and one hour, depending upon the time spent at each station.

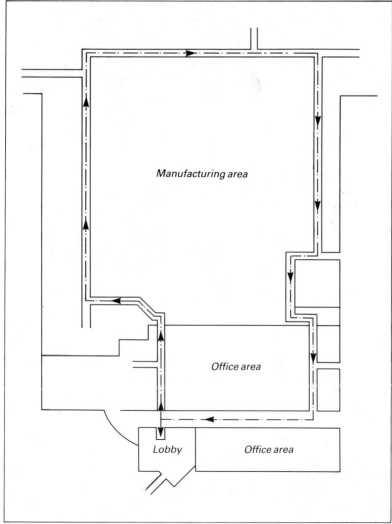

Fig. 16.8   Westinghouse guidepath layout

Some of the benefits derived include a safer environment for Westinghouse customers in the manufacturing area, an environment in which each person can easily hear the tour-guide speak, and reinforcement of the company's advanced 'high-tech' image. The personnel involved with the vehicle were all pleased with its performance and what it had accomplished.

AGVs in the US Postal Service*

To facilitate the movement of mail in the USA, the US Postal Service has over 200 major mail-processing facilities, general mail facilities (GMF) recognisable as large city post offices, and 21 bulk mail centres (BMC) (normally located in industrial parks) for sorting of sacks of mail and parcels. The US Postal Service is the second largest employer in the USA and literally handles millions of items of mail each day. Many of these facilities operate 24 hours a day, every day of the year, and range in floor-space between 200,000 and 3.5 million ft^2 (18,600–325,000m^2).

These mail-processing facilities require the movement of tons of mail over hundreds of feet between the inbound docks, the various processing areas, and the outbound docks. This involves moving the mail directly from the dock into the building, distribution throughout the floor area according to the type of mail, and then movement to the outbound docks. This must be done with a minimum of staging and no warehousing or storage.

Based on the throughput required, large gross weights over long distances, time restraints, and the fact that the Postal Service needed to keep existing wheeled containers, it was decided to incorporate tractor-type AGVs. Nationally, the Postal Service has an inventory of various types of wheeled containers worth billions of dollars, and obviously it is necessary to continue to use them. These containers are classified functionally as those suited for transport by truck or rail, those limited for use within the facility (such as large or small canvas hampers), and a third group that is not suitable for use with an AGV tractor system. There are a total of five containers suitable to be pulled in an AGV train and the mixing of containers in a train was determined to be acceptable; however, the number of each type of container and the total per train is set.

In these facilities, the floor-space is crucial, so aisles needed for the people and the AGV trains had to be kept to a minimum area compatible with safety. Thus, tracking accuracy of the trains of containers was a major consideration in the layout and width of aisles. To prevent loss of control of the train alignment from impacts upon stopping, it was essential that towing coupler provisions be integral to the containers, with controlled clearances

---

*This case study is based on a paper presented by Emerson W. Smith at the AGVS '85 Seminar, The Material Handling Institute. Emerson W. Smith is the General Manager – Engineering Division, Eastern Region US Postal Service, Philadelphia, Pennsylvania.

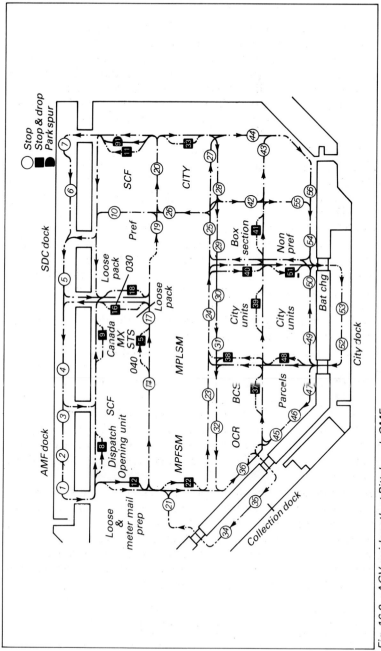

Fig. 16.9   AGV guidepath at Pittsburgh GMF

in the connections. Since it was not practical to update the inventory of all containers with integral towing provisions, each tractor is equipped to carry ten towbars for use with unmodified containers.

In addition, the AGV tractor was required to be able to control the opening of doors and the doors were required to close automatically behind the last container of the train to minimise loss of heat from the building. Also, off-guidepath manual operation of the tractors was required. This can be done either by an on-board driver or through the use of a hand-held pendant. Initially the AGV system specification called for a train of 10,000lb (approx. 4500kg) rolling gross weight, but experience has shown that greater efficiency is obtained by having more frequent moves at a lower gross weight of 6000lb (approx. 2700kg).

The Postal Service's demands on the AGV system are not like those of other industries where the demands are more uniform. The requirements for tractor movement of mail vary widely depending on the time of day. Although tractors are operated 20 hours per day, their activity approaches system capacity for inbound mail from about 4–8pm and for outbound mail from 2–6am. Mail-flow between operations within the workroom is continuous, making the duty cycle a composite.

Fig. 16.10   Tugger system at Pittsburgh GMF

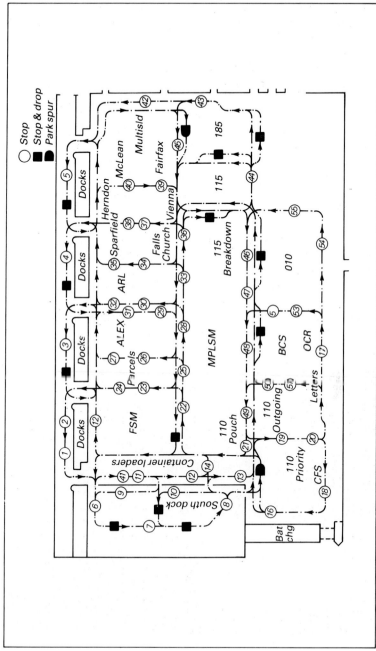

Fig. 16.11 AGV guidepath at Northern Virginia ℰMF

The AGV systems have been installed in five facilities. The first was a Raymond Electrotote System at the Syracuse GMF (General Mail Facility) in Syracuse, New York in 1979. It was expanded a few months later. The second system, also Raymond, was installed in the Hampton Road GMF at Norfolk, Virginia. The other systems are installed in the Buffalo GMF, New York, Pittsburgh GMF, Pennsylvania, and the Northern Virginia GMF, Merrifield, Virginia.

The Pittsburgh GMF is a new facility which was opened with the AGV system installed by Control Engineering Company of Jervis B. Webb. Fig. 16.9 shows its guidepath covering an 800 × 520ft (approx. 244 × 158m) workroom, using approximately 6500ft (approx. 2000m) of guidepath, with 56 stops and served by 12 tractors. Fig. 16.10 shows the tugger system. Two years of experience with the guidepath led to a number of changes in the original layout. These include the elimination of six drops and the addition of three more tractors to increase the system capacity.

A Barrett Electronics Corporation of Mannesmann Demag AGV system was installed in the existing Northern Virginia GMF, Merrifield, Virginia. The guidepath for this facility is shown in Fig. 16.11 and the actual tugger system is shown in Fig. 16.12.

Fig. 16.12   Tugger system at Northern Virginia GMF

In summary:

It should be obvious after reading this chapter that AGV systems are being readily accepted in non-manufacturing industries. Hospitals, offices, grocery distribution warehouses and postal services are just a few of the industries that already use AGVs in their facilities. As with all applications, unique problems exist, but experience has shown they can be overcome. In general, the system users seem pleased with their systems, and employee acceptance appears good.

Chapter Seventeen

Heavy duty applications for AGVs

M ost applications using unit load carriers have maximum load capacities of 5000–10,000lb (2268–4536kg). However, there is considerable interest in vehicles that can carry loads of up to 150,000lb (68040kg). This chapter is limited to applications that fall in this range of 10,000–150,000lb and the vehicles are referred to as 'heavy duty'.

Potential applications

Heavy duty vehicles are relatively new and very few actual applications exist but there is considerable interest in future applications in several types of industries. One of the more readily identifiable applications for heavy duty AGVs is in the metal stamping industry. AGVs would be used to move coils of steel from the storage areas to the blanking line and to move blanks from either the blanking press or storage area to the stamping line. Another application in this same industry is the movement of dies. It is not uncommon for a press line to consist of up to five or more individual presses and to be used to produce many different parts. Since some plants may contain many press lines, there can be several hundred dies in use. When a die is not in use, it needs to be stored somewhere, usually in a die storage area to prevent congestion around the press line. Also, dies require constant maintenance and checking, and so require transportation to the tool and die shop which is normally located in a different section of the plant. It is not uncommon for large dies to measure as much as 16 × 12 × 8ft (4.88 × 3.66 × 2.44m) and weigh up to 150,000lb

(68040kg). The tool and die shop could also use the AGVs to move unfinished dies from one machining operation to another.

Steel producing industries can use heavy duty AGVs for transporting steel coils, pre-cut blanks, and raw steel from one area to another or from one operation to another. In foundry operations, these vehicles can be used to move heavy castings, casting moulds, and ingots from the casting area to storage, between machining operations, or to shipping areas.

Other applications include moving heavy materials to assembly or machining operations, from one machining operation to another, or using them as assembly work-in-progress transporters. Examples of heavy production items include large diesel engines, large electrical transformers, aircraft, and military vehicles such as tanks or armoured personnel carriers. The AGVs can also become movable work platforms on which equipment can be mounted. This could be useful when the product is so large that it is not practical to move it (e.g. ships and locomotives). In these cases, it is easier to move the machine to the product than the product to the machine. It is possible to mount a robot or other machine on the vehicle to perform tasks, although many problems are

Fig. 17.1   Robot mounted on top of AGV

associated with such a feat (Fig. 17.1). Problems include positioning the vehicle accurately with respect to the workpiece, power consumption of the robot or other work platform equipment, and increased complexity of programming.

One final area of considerable interest are heavy duty AGVs that handle newsprint rolls. These special-purpose vehicles transport rolls of paper from the receiving dock to the press rooms of newspapers. They can be designed to interface with storage racks along with a wide variety of processing machines. With these potential applications in mind, the possibilities become almost limitless. Several AGV suppliers are now offering heavy duty vehicles so these potential applications can often be realised.

Special considerations

There are some special items that need to be taken into account when heavy duty AGVs are being considered. An important item is the floor condition, which is especially significant if the AGV is carrying unusually heavy loads. Foreign material, such as oil or sand, can be detrimental to the guidance, wheels, and possibly even communication of the vehicles. The heavy loads may cause the floors to deflect, causing the guidewire and communication loop wires to fail or come in contact with metal reinforcement rods.

Another consideration is the turning envelope of the vehicle. Since heavy duty vehicles are usually very large, their turning radius can be significant. To allow for this (plus a safety margin to eliminate pinch points) aisle widths and intersections may have to be modified. Even though the combined payload and vehicle weight may be much greater than that of typical vehicles found on most AGV systems, the safety considerations must remain the same. For example, the vehicle must be able to stop within the safety bumper deflection. At the same time, during the deceleration and stopping of the vehicle, the load must be prevented from shifting.

Special work platforms must be designed to accommodate the loads. When loads such as coils of steel weighing several tens of thousands of pounds are being carried, the work platform must not allow the coils to shift position or roll off. At the same time the vehicle should be able to accept coils of varying widths and diameters. If the coils are to be automatically loaded and unloaded, there must be precision locating of the coils on the work

Fig. 17.2 Work platform for carrying coil steel and blanks

platform, as well as the ability to locate the vehicle precisely with respect to the load/unload mechanisms. Loading and unloading blanks automatically will require a different approach, such as powered rollers or some kind of push/pull mechanism. Fig. 17.2 illustrates an example of a work platform.

Fig. 17.3 Vehicle carrying dies

For the press line, it would be desirable to be able to carry dies automatically in and out of the press. The dies would be transferred between the AGVs and the presses without human aid (Fig. 17.3). This requires that the rolling bolster, which is an integral part of the press, and the AGV work platform be the same height and that the AGV has a mechanism powerful enough to push and pull the dies either off or on, as required.

The final special consideration is the high cost of these heavy duty vehicles. One of the major reasons they are making such a slow impact in industry is their high cost. Heavy duty AGVs are still in their early stage of development, with every application requiring custom design and manufacturing. The development cost of the prototype vehicles considerably increases the cost of the system to be purchased. Cost should decrease as experience is gained. However, systems can often be justified for other than purely economic reasons, such as the elimination of dull, demanding, routine, and dangerous jobs.

Case studies

The following four case studies are based on material supplied by Michael Urban, Director of Marketing, Mentor Products, Inc., Mentor, Ohio.

Ford Motor Company – Maumee Stamping Plant

The Ford Metal Stamping Division at Maumee, Ohio will employ the most modern and sophisticated computer integrated manufacturing techniques available. One of the integral tools of this facility is the sheet-metal blank handling AGV system developed by Mentor. The purpose of the system is to deliver palletised blanks to the head of the draw press line from which doors, hoods, side panels, and other stamped parts are formed.

The coil steel is uncoiled and sheered into rectangular blanks. These blanks are either delivered by the AGVs to the press line or to the storage area for later use. The stacks of blanks are up to 60in. (approx. 152cm) wide, 100in. (approx. 254cm) in length, and 15,000lb (approx. 6800kg) in weight. The conveyors used to unload the blanks are generally 12in. (approx. 30.5cm) off the floor, while some conveyors at the head of the draw press lines are as high as 48in. (approx. 122cm). The AGV (Fig. 17.4) is required to interface with both conveyor systems. To accomplish this, the

Fig. 17.4   Ford Maumee Stamping Plant's AGV

AGV was built with a ball screw lift table that varies in height from 12 to 48in. off the floor. The AGV table has powered rollers to match the powered off-board conveyors.

An order for a pallet of blanks is generated when the wait station for blanks at the draw press line becomes vacant. The AGV system is designed to deliver a pallet of blanks within 5min of receiving the request. The expected results of this system are elimination of damage to blanks during handling, better press utilisation, safety, and savings over traditional manual methods.

Manufacturing rocket fuel

A major aerospace contractor is building a facility to manufacture rocket fuel. The highly volatile and explosive operations are being constructed high in the mountains. The fuel is combined in a giant mixing bowl, $10ft^2$ (approx. $3.5m^2$) at the base and 14ft (approx. 4.3m) high. Each ingredient of the fuel is added to the mixing bow in separate buildings. The buildings are spread over a linear area of more than 4000ft (approx. 1220m) to avoid damage to any sites in the event of an accidental explosion.

To carry the mixing bowl from one process building to another, a Mentor AGV will be used. When full, the mixing bowl weighs 70,000lb (approx. 31,500kg). An on-board load of 105,000lb (approx. 47,250kg) is required during the try-out test period. The AGVs will be inherently safe with a diesel engine and pump delivering explosion-proof hydraulic fluid to two giant drive wheels. The drive wheels differentially turn to provide steering (similar to a bulldozer).

A few of the mixing process buildings have lead-shielded floors, making buried wire guidance impossible. In these areas, the AGV will be guided with a vision system and passive targets located to obtain accurate vehicle positioning. An on-board VAX computer will handle the artificial intelligence software required for the exceptionally high-speed computing. The system controller will consist of two Micro VAX II computers, one acting as a back-up for the other.

Because of the hazardous environment, the long runs of travel, the heavy payloads, and the computer-control requirements, AGVs are the ideal choice for this material-handling operation.

GM-BOC – Kalamazoo, Michigan

The BOC Kalamazoo Metal Stamping Plant is restructuring the method currently used in the manufacturing of stamping dies. This is part of its 'tool-room modernisation' programme. Throughput requirements have made the use of overhead cranes impossible, so alternative methods were investigated. A Mentor AGV system was selected since it will permit the die manufacturing process time to be reduced considerably to meet the required throughput.

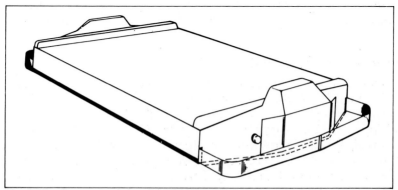

Fig. 17.5   Conceptual sketch of GM-BOC Kalamazoo's AGV

The AGVs selected will be able to transport 60,000lb (approx. 27,000kg) dies through an FMS. The raw castings and fixture are mounted on air-bearing pallets which are floated onto the vehicle on a cushion of air (shop air). The vehicle then transports the casting, pallet and fixture to one of 21 horizontal machining centres and workstations. To obtain positional accuracies of 1mm, the vehicle stops and sets itself down over cones at the machining centres. This is accomplished by releasing air from air bags on board. The vehicle has a unique extractor device for pushing the load off or pulling the load on, as required. Fig. 17.5 shows a conceptual sketch of the vehicle. The system is due to be installed in mid-1986.

Robotic application

Cybotech Corporation has designed and built a huge horizontal arm robot which rides on a Mentor AGV (Fig. 17.6). This unit will be used to paint machinery for a classified military aerospace programme. The six-axis robot weighs 7.5 tons (approx. 6800kg) is 25ft (approx. 7.6m) tall and has a reach of 15ft (approx. 4.6m).

Fig. 17.6 Cybotech robot mounted on Mentor AGV

This unit could also be used for painting large parts, such as commercial or military aircraft and other military vehicles. It can also be used for welding large parts, such as components for naval ships, buses, off-road equipment, and various military vehicles.

In summary:

It is now possible to transport very heavy loads up to 150,000lb (approx. 68040kg) by AGVs. Vehicles with these large-load capacities are being used to handle steel, clay model cars, and TNT. Heavy duty vehicles are a relatively new extension of AGVs; thus, caution should be exercised when considering their use. Because of their expense, other than purely economic consideration may be necessary to justify their use. However, the use of these vehicles exhibits promise for application in many types of industries.

Chapter Eighteen

Future trends

A lthough it is difficult to predict the future with absolute certainty, we can concentrate on the trends that seem to indicate the future status of AGV systems. By talking with suppliers and users, and reading technical papers on AGV systems, we can see that certain trends are definitely indicative.

Indicated trends

Guidance

At present, vehicles can leave the guidepath for short distances, and by using deadreckoning control, find their destination and return to the guidepath. Much research is being accomplished to expand this capability and even to eliminate the need for guidance using a guidepath (wire or optical). As discussed in Chapter Six, both inertial and pattern recognition guidance techniques show much promise.

There are three major obstacles to a quicker acceptance of these new guidance techniques: firstly, in most industrial environments, wire-guidance techniques are acceptable; secondly, wire guidance has proven its reliability even in harsh environments; and thirdly, because of these two factors, any new guidance technology must be cost comparable or be far superior in its capabilities to warrant the extra expense. The obvious advantage will be for those industries that require continual system modification.

On-board controllers

On-board controllers are rapidly becoming considerably more sophisticated, and at the same time they are becoming smaller and less expensive. The vehicle controllers are exhibiting such features as expanded diagnostics. Although the vehicles cannot repair themselves, they can at least indicate their problems to the maintenance or repair personnel. The more sophisticated the diagnostics, the more likely the repairs will be able to be made quickly. Associated with this is that maintenance is being made simpler by the use of plug-in cards and control units, so it becomes a matter of quick component exchange.

Controller sophistication will also allow the vehicle to operate more intelligently in complex handling situations and will increase the system integrity in the event of a host-computer failure. The vehicles will be able to exhibit more flexible path programming, allowing alternate routes for faster material movements and greater throughput. It is possible to have certain guidepaths limited to high-speed motion, with the controller being able to merge the vehicle into high-speed traffic.

Vehicle communications

The trend is toward continuous as opposed to discrete communication so that the vehicle will be able to communicate and receive updated instructions at any time. There will also be increased communications between the vehicles and the workstation automation. The vehicles must be able to interface readily with other automation, especially as industries move toward the automated factory.

System controllers

Systems will be designed to have increased capability to track material and store this information. For example, they will be able to follow and control material flow to support just-in-time concepts. The system controllers will also be able to be integrated into the MAP network allowing it to communicate with any of the other facility controllers. There will probably be more standardisation of both the control hardware and software.

Vehicles

There will be continued growth in the use of AGVs in assembly processes. As more is learned of how to take full advantage of asynchronous parallel path processing, interest in AGV systems for assembly operations will increase. Vehicles will become more standardised, requiring less engineering to adapt the vehicle to a particular task, thus lowering the cost of the vehicles. This will make them easier to justify for many users. It will be more like purchasing an automobile: order the basic vehicle and add the necessary standard off-the-shelf options to configure the vehicle to meet specific needs. Other areas where considerable interest and growth are likely include FMS, heavy-load vehicles for stamping operations and die shops, and light-load vehicles for electronics manufacturing, especially clean-room environments.

Batteries

More interest in maintenance-free batteries and an increased trend to opportunity charging are likely. This will be feasible since such applications as assembly and FMS readily support opportunity charging. For material-handling applications using tuggers or fork-type trucks, there will be vast improvements in deep-cycle battery capabilities as well as overall battery life.

Improved graphical displays

There will probably be increased use of colour graphical displays showing the entire guidepath, every vehicle location, the vehicle identification, the vehicle status, the vehicle load and its status, and possibly even the status of the automation interfaced to the AGV system. Use of a menu driven touch screen will make the display user-friendly.

Robots on AGVs

More applications will be developed using robots mounted on AGVs. This will increase the capability of both as it gives the robot the mobility it lacks and the AGV the flexible manipulator it lacks. This will be particularly useful in hazardous environments, such as the handling of nuclear materials. Other areas of interest include FMS interfacing with various machine-tool operations and automatic order picking in warehousing situations. Major problem areas associated with this are how to carry sufficient battery power for both the AGV and the robot and also the packaging required (especially the controls). Some people are predicting a totally robotic high-rise lift truck for low-rise warehouses of 20–25ft (approx. 6.1–7.6m). This type of vehicle would be of great value to grocery distribution warehouses where orders have to be made up for small local grocery stores.

Simulation

Special-purpose simulation languages will continue to become user-friendly and the cost of simulation will also decrease. Graphics will play a more important role, with improved colour graphics input and display systems integrated directly into simulation languages and simulation output processors. Integrated databases will link to factory database input for more comprehensive output analysis.

Safety

Although safety has not been a problem with AGV systems, there is considerable concern. New safety sensors for proximity (non-contact obstacle) detection will be developed and coupled with the increased computing power of the on-board controller to produce an even safer vehicle that can readily negotiate a pedestrian-clogged aisle. This will be of utmost importance to non-manufacturing environments such as hospitals and offices.

AGV acceptance

As AGV systems are successfully implemented into various applications and environments, the results of these systems will become known to others. Awareness of the improved quality of work-life and ergonomics, resulting from the use of AGVs, will create more acceptance on the part of the labour force and the unions. Likewise, awareness of such advantages as asynchronous processing, increased product quality, fewer damaged parts, and better inventory control will create more interest and acceptance by management. Such increased acceptance can only help promote considerable growth in the AGV industry.

In summary:

If the trends discussed in this chapter continue as they have done in the last few years, there should be considerable growth in the use of AGV systems in both manufacturing and non-manufacturing environments. Hopefully this book has increased the reader's knowledge of AGV systems, their merits and limitations, and will encourage the prospective user into considering the use of AGVs as a material-handling system.

References

[1] Productivity through automated guided vehicles. Paper presented at *AGV Tutorial, Robots 9 Conf.* Robotics International of SME, Detroit, June 1985.

[2] Koff, G.A. and Boldrin, B. 1985. Automated guided vehicles. *Materials Handling Handbook,* Ch. 8. Wiley Interscience.

[3] Adams, W.P. Automated guided vehicle systems. *Automated Material Handling and Storage,* 5.1.1 – 5.1.12. Auerbach Publishers Inc.

[4] *Facts and Fixes,* Maintenance and Repair of the Volvo AutoCarrier System. Volvo of America Corporation, 1984.

[5] Beck, E.D. 1983. *A Layman's Guide to Control Systems Design.* SPS Technologies, Hatfield, Pennsylvania.

[6] Premi, S.K. and Besant, C.B. 1983. A review of various vehicle guidance techniques that can be used by mobile robots or AGVS. In, *Proc. 2nd Int. Conf. on Automated Guided Vehicle Systems,* pp. 195-209. IFS (Publications) Ltd, Bedford, UK.

[7] Taylor, D. 1985. A simulation overview. In, *GM 1985 Seminar on AGVS.* Lansing, Michigan.

[8] Turner, D.H. and Quinn, M.E. 1985. Advanced AGVS simulation. In, *Automated Guided Vehicle Systems.* Society of Manufacturing Engineers, Dearborn, Michigan.

[9] Dewsnup, M.C. 1985. Simulation of integrated systems. In, *Proc. ProMat 85, an MHI International Show and Forum,* pp. 18-23. Chicago, Illinois.

[10] Turner, D.H. 1984. Simulation in factory automation. Paper presented at *AIIE November Dinner Meeting,* Frankenmuth, 1984.

[11] *AGVS Industry Applications.* Material Handling Institute, Inc. 1983.

[12] Automatic guided vehicles: Installing standalone AGV systems in existing plant layouts. *Plant Engineering,* August 15, 1985, pp. 86-7.

GARY C. HAMMOND is a consultant and partner of Robotic Integrated Systems Engineering, Inc. (RISE). Prior to this he was a professor of Mechanical Engineering at GMI Engineering & Management Institute in Flint, Michigan, where he taught for 21 years. He has a BS in Mechanical Engineering from Michigan Technological University and an MS from Ohio State University. Before GMI he was an officer in the US Air Force, working on the space programme at Vanderberg AFB, California, and worked as a dynamics engineer for North American Aviation.

Mr. Hammond has specialised in the areas of experimental stress analysis, electronic instrumentation, and sensor development. He is a recognised specialist in the area of instrumentation and sensors and served many years on the GM Instrumentation Subcommittee. He has also authored much text material used at GMI and within GM on the subject of instrumentation, including sensor and transducer development.

For the past few years Mr. Hammond has been involved in robotics, robotic systems, automated guided vehicles and flexible automation, and has participated in the development of the GMI Robotics Center. He has also been instrumental in the development of several robotic courses including basics, applications, and integrated manufacturing systems (advanced manufacturing concepts). He has made numerous presentations on various robotic subjects and automated guided vehicles and has been involved in many consulting efforts concerned with robotic and flexible automation systems. He has also served as a member of the GM Robotic Test & Evaluation Subcommittee.

Mr. Hammond is also a member of the Education and Training Division of Robotics International of SME and serves as a member on several other SME committees.